EMILY BRONTË:
WUTHERING HEIGHTS

by

J. F. GOODRIDGE

Reader in English
The University of Lancaster

EDWARD ARNOLD

© J. F. GOODRIDGE 1964

First published 1964
by Edward Arnold (Publishers) Ltd
41 Bedford Square, London WC1B 3DQ

Reprinted 1967, 1968, 1971, 1977, 1979

ISBN: 0 7131 5376 8

To John Watts
to whom I am indebted for help and criticism

Printed and bound in Great Britain at
The Camelot Press Ltd, Southampton

Contents

General Preface

The object of this series is to provide studies of individual novels, plays and groups of poems and essays which are known to be widely read by students. The emphasis is on clarification and evaluation; biographical and historical facts, while they may be discussed when they throw light on particular elements in a writer's work, are generally subordinated to critical discussion. What kind of work is this? What exactly goes on here? How good is this work, and why? These are the questions that each writer will try to answer.

It should be emphasized that these studies are written on the assumption that the reader has already read carefully the work discussed. The objective is not to enable students to deliver opinions about works they have not read, nor is it to provide ready-made ideas to be applied to works that have been read. In one sense all critical interpretation can be regarded as foisting opinions on readers, but to accept this is to deny the advantages of any sort of critical discussion directed at students or indeed at anybody else. The aim of these studies is to provide what Coleridge called in another context 'aids to reflection' about the works discussed. The interpretations are offered as suggestive rather than as definitive, in the hope of stimulating the reader into developing further his own insights. This is after all the function of all critical discourse among sensible people.

Because of the interest which this kind of study has aroused, it has been decided to extend it first from merely English literature to include also some selected works of American literature and now further to include selected works in English by Commonwealth writers. The criterion will remain that the book studied is important in itself and is widely read by students.

DAVID DAICHES

'But these passions and thoughts and feelings are the general passions and thoughts and feelings of men. And with what are they connected? Undoubtedly with our moral sentiments and animal sensations, and with the causes which excite these; with the operations of the elements, and the appearances of the visible universe, with storm and sunshine, with the revolutions of the seasons, with cold and heat. . . .'

Wordsworth, Preface to *Lyrical Ballads*

'It is not without reason
That this hollow
Has been put away in a wilderness.
It means
That the place of love
Lies not in beaten ways
Nor about our human dwellings.
Love haunts the deserts.
The road that leads to its retreat
Is a hard and toilsome road.'

Gottfried von Strassburg, *Tristan*

'Love seeketh not Itself to please,
'Nor for itself hath any care,
'But for another gives its ease,
'And builds a Heaven in Hell's despair' . . .

'Love seeketh only Self to please,
'To bind another to Its delight,
'Joys in another's loss of ease,
'And builds a Hell in Heaven's despite.'

William Blake, *The Clod and the Pebble*

1. The Overture

The purpose of this commentary is to help the student towards a closer reading of *Wuthering Heights* as a *novel*. It is necessary to say this because there is a tendency to regard it as anything but a novel—a personal document, a fairytale or myth, a mystical poem, a Yorkshire curio or a study in the psychology of maladjustment. The one essential attribute of a good novel, according to Henry James, is that it should possess that 'air of reality' which he defines as 'solidity of specification'.[1] Our aim here must be to see as clearly as possible what kind of 'reality' the novel presents, and to look steadily at the whole pattern.

To do this, we must constantly bear in mind that Nelly Dean defines her two narratives as 'the history of Mr. Heathcliff'—not the romance of the two Catherines. This 'history' forms the main body of the novel, and Brontë's presentment of Heathcliff is therefore the central problem in any critical study. Is Heathcliff sufficiently convincing as hero of the story? Mr. Derek Stanford[2] thinks not: 'Heathcliff', he writes, 'is situated right in the centre of the drama. And yet he is, truly, less plausible than Lockwood. His reality is that of a lay figure. . . . He appears to have a powerful inner life, just as Cathy, Hareton and Catherine do; and it is only when we reconsider him that we feel a lack of flexibility, a sense of internal development missing.'

This is a challenging criticism which no commentator can avoid. I shall try in this study to provide some pointers by which readers may be enabled to answer it for themselves.

1. Inspecting the Penetralium (I-II)

The date, 1801, provides a point of reference not too near, nor yet too remote in time for a mid-nineteenth-century reader. The immediately recognisable form, a personal diary, establishes for us an easy intimacy with an impartial character whose style—self-conscious, a little affected

[1] *The House of Fiction* (Mercury Books): The Art of Fiction, 1884.

[2] Muriel Spark and Derek Stanford, *Emily Brontë, Her Life and Work* (Peter Owen, 1960).

and facetious—is nicely calculated to engage sympathy while allowing the reader ground for ironic detachment, even amusement at the narrator's expense. The hackneyed language ('a beautiful country . . . a perfect misanthropist's heaven . . . a capital fellow') lulls us into the complacent attitude of a city gentleman towards the country—and then, at once, the dramatic confrontation with Heathcliff.

There is no set description of him, only movements, gestures, dialogue. The verbs suggest something more than ordinary reserve—a physical recoil from human contact, like an animal's into its shell—'black eyes withdraw . . . fingers sheltered . . . wincing . . . closed teeth.'

Lockwood's curiosity is aroused and he becomes alert. We now take in the essential details of the house through his sharp, intelligent observation: first, the lack of servants, the neglect of the farm and the sour hostility of Joseph; then its significant name and the brief, telling details that reveal its exposed position along with its massive strength, its antiquity and family name. As soon as Lockwood gets his eye on the object, the language and rhythm of his prose is shaped economically to express the precise quality of the thing seen—'a range of gaunt thorns all stretching their limbs one way, as if craving alms of the sun'.

Heathcliff's peremptory attitude silences Lockwood's sightseeing enquiries. One step though, and his keen eye is 'inspecting the penetralium': depth and emptiness, a strange absence of the usual signs of domesticity in a large country household; massive, inhuman, antiquated furniture; bare, functional architecture; the inert signs of a once cheerful, though primitive way of life; and the great towering dresser, its dark recesses now 'haunted' by savage dogs.

Already sensing something wrong in the picture, Lockwood tries to superimpose on it the homely elements he misses. But Heathcliff, foreign-looking—a dark-skinned gypsy though 'in dress and manners a gentleman'—is emphatically *there*. Lockwood must, somehow, assimilate him to his own conventional likeness: so he 'runs on', 'bestowing his own attributes' on him, trying to interpret him in the light of his own facile social foibles.

The attack by the dogs dramatises Lockwood's incongruous efforts to come to terms with 'Wuthering Heights' and its grim landlord. He attempts to caress them, and they turn out to be 'fiends', 'possessed swine', 'a brood of tigers'. Heathcliff growls 'in unison' with them. He has never tamed them: the bitch is 'not kept for a pet'.

The inert, antique furniture has revealed a secret life: savagery and fiendishness issuing from its 'hidden dens'. But Heathcliff is shrewd: not wishing to lose a tenant, he makes his guest forget what he has seen. Lockwood is again attracted, and the reader alternates with him between attraction and repulsion. His return the next day is compulsive: he *will* couple himself with Heathcliff and find in him an *alter ego*.

In II the weather of the Heights seems to conspire in the attack on Lockwood's composure. Its air makes him 'shiver in every limb'. The chapter is filled with information, all of which Lockwood, still disorientated, ludicrously misunderstands. We are looking, first, at a collage—every detail sharply focussed, the whole gradually combining to create 'a dismal spiritual atmosphere', but the pieces still refusing to fit into a consistent whole.

Every detail is *used*: there is no lumber. Even the two painted canisters mentioned in I now perform an important function, providing the dramatic occasion for Lockwood's scrutiny of Mrs. Heathcliff. And every image, almost every word, here, is taken up and given a vital function later in the novel.[1]

Brontë never dwells for long on any one object; hers is never a static picture; each detail is set in motion—everything interacts. The eye moves from person to person, and each encounter is presented as a miniature scene in a continuous drama of frustration. First, we see Joseph's head framed in a round barn window, and hear for the first time his characteristic tone and dialect—uncouth, gnarled and impenetrably harsh and resistant. Then Mrs. Heathcliff, proof against all advances, whose sudden metamorphosis into a beautiful fairy girl when she moves into the light ('slender . . . exquisite . . . small . . . flaxen ringlets . . . delicate') makes her scornful insouciance towards Lockwood more shocking and unaccountable.

(One of the most significant techniques which Brontë employs throughout the novel is this of *metamorphosis*—the sudden shift of perspective that turns a voice, a physical presence, a person or thing into a being quite different from the one we expected.)

Then the physical reality of the brutish Hareton bears down upon us with oppressive vividness. Only Dickens can rival Brontë in this rendering of a physical presence.

[1] Consider, for example, 'fairy' and 'witch' in connection with Joseph's attitude to Cathy in XXXIII: 'It's yon flaysome, graceless quean, that's witched our lad, wi' her bold een. . . .'

The multiple humorous and ironic contrasts in these opening chapters only reveal themselves after repeated readings. Notice, for example, the various ways in which Lockwood's youthful attitudes—the picture he gives us of his own reserve, his failure in love and interest in Cathy, etc.—serve to emphasise the real ferocity of the passions that are smouldering in the household. There is the promise of friendliness in the warmth and comfort of the apartment with its immense fire, followed by brutal inhospitality. There is the extraordinary childishness, side by side with a hard-bitten, passionate vindictiveness in Mrs. Heathcliff, and the fact (which Lockwood tries not to believe) that Joseph trembles 'with sincere horror' at her threats of witchcraft. More important still, there is the sudden revelation of Heathcliff's real savagery and hatred towards her, which makes Lockwood 'no longer . . . inclined to call him a capital fellow'.

As Lockwood beats about in this maze, the weather turns to 'one bitter whirl of wind and suffocating snow' (who but Brontë could make us sense its power in so few words?). In the uproar of contradictory words, physical assaults, shouts, roars of laughter and recriminations, all Lockwood's inner and outer composure is destroyed.

In Brontë, the effect of confusion is compounded of a series of sharp, distinct sensations. The contradictions and bewilderments are not, as in James or Conrad, partly subjective: they are real, they belong to the nature of things.

2. *The Inner Recesses* (III)

Lockwood is now sick, dizzy, faint, all his efforts to resist the shock of new impressions overcome. He unwittingly allows himself to be led deeper into the penetralium of the house—the forbidden chamber whose ancient oak will prove to be alive with the mystery of Heathcliff and Catherine. He thinks himself secure in the oak closet, but the names on the ledge, and the intenser reality of Catherine's diary, leap at him: 'An immediate interest *kindled* within me for the unknown Catherine.'

Catherine's entry in the book provides a transparent window into the past, bringing it closer than the present. Her tone is intense with a whispered, seething passion of defiance. (Notice, in the first paragraph, the hissing sibilants in a succession of short main clauses following one another in urgent succession.) The style is literate but unselfconscious, and has the immediacy and directness of a child's writing under a great stress of feeling.

This is not just a typical day in the childhood of Catherine and Heathcliff, but a crucial one. As Arnold Kettle has said,[1] the love of Catherine and Heathcliff is born in rebellion: 'Heathcliff and I are going to rebel—we took our initiatory step this evening.' This step, of throwing the books which represented the puritan way to heaven into the dog-kennel, means a rejection of the only form of Christianity they know, the religion of Joseph. (It is clear that Catherine was the ringleader; but for her, Heathcliff might have remained forever impassive.) The rebellion also leads directly to the fateful scamper to Thrushcross Grange described in Heathcliff's narrative (VI).

Catherine's expression of contempt for Hindley's 'paradise' of kissing and baby-talk on the hearth marks out the direction (not infantile) that her love for Heathcliff will take. The brief postscript where she weeps for his degradation has a similar function: it marks a point of crystallisation in her love for him, which will determine its quality once it becomes a self-conscious passion. It is to be in essence a sharing of his miseries—his outcast, vagabond life: 'My great miseries in the world have been Heathcliff's miseries, and I watched and felt each *from the beginning.*' (IX)

The main elements of Lockwood's nightmare—Branderham's sermon and its association with Joseph, the snow, the chapel he had passed on his walks, the physical assault on his person, the child Catherine associated with the window-ledge, the sound of storm and tapping branch—are already present in his fevered imagination before they coalesce. And partly for this reason the new, realistic horror of the 'ice-cold hand', the voice that replied 'shiveringly', the child's face and, above all, the wrist rubbed on the broken pane 'till the blood ran down and soaked the bedclothes', is all the more startling.

The dream of Branderham's sermon is preposterous, and appropriate enough for Lockwood, to put us off our guard. Its significance for the reader lies in the idea of the dissolution of both church and chapel, here coalesced into one. The decaying, ministerless kirk is now the home only of embalmed corpses. The chapel, with its Calvinistic gibberish of sin and damnation, has taken its place. Joseph and all the people flock to hear a sermon on a text (Matt. xviii, 21-2) which teaches a boundless love and forgiveness of neighbours, but which is transformed by the

[1] *Introduction to the English Novel*, Vol. I, Part III, v (Hutchinson University Library).

homilectic method of subdivision into a diatribe which makes the number of sins seem infinite; each one bringing us nearer to the point where, through an absurd numerical literalism, forgiveness and mercy run out and are transformed into vengeance. In Joseph's world, Christianity is a religion of mutual damnation, where 'every man's hand is against his neighbour'.

The mad tumult of religious conflict having passed away, we are left with only the wailing blast and the rattling of dry cones. Lockwood is only half asleep, since he knows where he is and is acutely aware of real sounds. Then the matter-of-fact narration—active verbs of muscular strain and shock—knock, stretch, close, draw back, cling, struggle, shake off, pull, rub—and the 'ghost's' refusal to give way after we should have expected Lockwood's terror to awake him; then more scratching and thrusting till he cries out.

Psychological explanations (telepathy) have only a partial relevance here. For the reader there is a sense of something palpable—forces at work in wind, storm and house as well as in Heathcliff's mind, beyond anything Lockwood's subconscious could conceive. He has tried to remain indifferent to the untamed realities of the Heights. Now they take their revenge on him. That *he* should be the subject, or victim, makes their reality more convincing. He is now a passive agent; only his terror, and consequent cruelty to the ghost-child, are his own.

Lockwood has sought Heathcliff's friendship and is now ironically placed in the position of an intruder into the deepest secrets of his life —as if, by some strange substitution, he himself had taken the place of Heathcliff by occupying the oak closet. He is mysteriously drawn into the recesses of Heathcliff's history and made a witness of his anguish.

Brontë's narrative is never loose or random in any given particular. Therefore it is relevant to ask precise questions: Why is the hook soldered into the staple? Why does she call herself *Linton* and not *Earnshaw*, since her face is that of a child? Is Heathcliff afraid of Catherine's ghost?

Heathcliff's replies to Lockwood's 'wild and whirling' words are typically stark and stiff. The impression he gives is of a man to whom the barest politeness, all cultivated speech, is a foreign mode forced out of him by an act of will. His natural speech would be like that of a wild beast. His words at the open lattice represent the barest expression of feeling one could put into words; if you alter Brontë's italics and emphasise the wrong words, they become flat and lifeless. Similarly, the physical symptoms in him of excessive feeling are raw and elemental —irregular breathing, an uncontrollable gush of tears. They are no more 'ham' than is the moaning of an animal.

The heavy, savage vehemence of Heathcliff's speech arises from a depth of passionate feeling that cannot express itself with the range and suppleness of rhythm, or the lyrical fervour, that Catherine has.[1] As a man he is not highly imaginative, but superstitious and literal-minded to the point of mania. His tragedy and final triumph (which in the supernatural realm, has something in common with that of Conrad's Captain McWhirr in the physical) lie partly in his taking all that Catherine says (and Lockwood's nightmare) literally.

The 'narrow lobbies' of the Heights allow no escape; there is no place for a stranger in this house; it resists foreigners, or else it draws them in completely. Its furnace-like open fires, fierce as the weather outside, come to symbolise for us its pent-up life, spitting sparks of hatred at Cathy as she tries to read. Joseph's 'sanctum', to which Lockwood is now forced to retreat, is closer to the bare life of the elements than Heathcliff's stone-flagged parlour. 'We cannot be damper, or colder, in the rain than we are here,' Catherine had said of this back-kitchen. But Joseph has now made it his lair. He is quite at home in this 'infernal house'; the parasite has become inseparable from the tree.

The nightmare is only one part of the total situation Brontë wishes to convey: a household which begins now to appear a self-consistent world. Before Lockwood can make his escape, we are given a more rounded picture of its callous domestic life. Each of its inmates hates and fears others attempting to invade his jealously guarded privacy.

Outside, in the 'free air' into which Lockwood escapes, the snow has obliterated all landmarks. We are made to realise here the vast extent of the 'barren' which separates 'Wuthering Heights' from the civilised world—deep bogs and pits ready to swallow up any unwary traveller. Lockwood arrives home 'benumbed to his very heart'.

This 'overture' forms a microcosm of the whole novel and is seminal to what follows. 'The three chapters', remarks Mr. T. Crehan,[2] 'present

---

[1] Cf. his last outcry in XVI, with the climax 'Oh, God! it is unutterable! . . .', etc.
[2] The London English Literature edition of *Wuthering Heights*, Commentary.

Heathcliff's agony, Cathy's misfortune, Catherine Earnshaw's devouring need and Hareton's ambiguous status of farm labourer-cum-rightful owner.' They also give us a number of different perspectives on Heathcliff which are already beginning to coalesce.

2. The Narrative Form, I

1. Multiple Perspectives

The viewpoint is transferred to a point within the picture, the picture thus gains in depth, and the light which illuminates it seems to come from within it.

Auerbach, *Mimesis*, II (on Petronius' *Fortunata*)

The whole action of *Wuthering Heights* is presented in the form of eye-witness narrations by people who have played some part in the events they describe. These narratives do not run parallel to one another like, for example, those in Browning's *The Ring and the Book*, but are closely fitted one inside the other, each opening out from its parent narrative to reveal a new stratum of the story.

Thus the narrative thread is unbroken throughout, in spite of its intricate structure of time shifts.[1] The value of this unified dramatic structure is clear if we compare *Wuthering Heights* with Anne Brontë's *The Tenant of Wildfell Hall*, where a similar technique of direct narration is employed clumsily for didactic purposes, without cohesion.

Lockwood's diary is the outer framework of the whole story. He is then present as the recipient of Nelly's story, and she in turn is the recipient of further 'tertiary' narratives—those of Heathcliff (VI and XXIX), Isabella (XIII and XVII), Cathy (XXIV) and Zillah (XXX). In fact Nelly's narrative is so fully dramatised that it is studded with lesser narratives. Almost all the events are recorded in the words of the participants; thus our perspective is constantly changing or being enlarged by a kind of twofold mirror.

Our reading of the opening chapters has shown how impossible it is to understand the household of the Heights from the point of view of a

---

[1] See the chart on p. 49.

normal outsider. The purpose of Brontë's narrative method is to draw the reader (as Lockwood was drawn into the penetralium of the house) into a position where he can only judge its events from within.

The strict conditions which Brontë's narrative form imposes upon her resemble those of poetic drama. She cannot speak in her own person; direct satire is therefore excluded, and there can be no irony except of a dramatic kind, inherent in the contradictions of the events themselves and the attitudes of the narrators. The story must speak entirely for itself; its values must be self-generated, created for us by the quality of the language especially in moments of strong feeling and self-revelation on the part of the protagonists.

When we read a novel like Jane Austen's *Emma*, we share very largely the detached, ironic point of view of the novelist. But since, in *Wuthering Heights*, each narrative takes place within the action, occupying an important place in its dramatic structure, the reader never stands completely outside the story. If this were not so, the dramatic impact of Brontë's narrow, remote world might be greatly diminished; everything in it looms very large because we experience it only from within.

All direct speech for Brontë is passionate communication,[1] illuminating some aspect of the speaker or situation; there is little place in her novel for polite small talk.

So the objective narrative contains within itself tragic personal histories which (as Catherine says of her dreams) go through us 'like wine through water, and alter the colour of [our] minds' (IX). While the larger framework of Lockwood's and Nelly's narratives provides the necessary objectivity, the smaller, more condensed and compelling personal narratives like Catherine's diary, which are embedded in them, give us direct glimpses into the inner imaginative lives of the main protagonists. These together form the core of the novel and are joined in subtle ways with one another. They appear suddenly out of the 'darkness of an unilluminated past' and always remain 'vibrant in the background',[2] modifying our view of all the outward events that Lockwood or Nelly describe. Catherine's delirious ravings (XII), for example, contain many such glimpses, forming imaginative links backwards and forwards as we read and resounding in our minds throughout the story. It is this resonance which gives us, in *Wuthering Heights*, a sense of

---

[1] Perhaps because in real life she spoke so little.
[2] Auerbach, op. cit., I.

B

Auerbach's 'tensional and suspensive striving towards a goal' as opposed to a mere succession of events. 'However far we penetrate', remarks Mr. Hillis Miller, 'towards the centre of *Wuthering Heights* there are still further recesses within.'[1]

2. Past and Present

Brontë seeks to engage the reader directly through the reactions of her narrators. Thus her technique is abrupt and dramatic, allowing us little time, on a first reading, for dispassionate contemplation. With no preliminary explanation she confronts us with a sharply focussed scene where the characters are realised first as physical presences. They are set in motion at once, the action mounts swiftly and unexpectedly, and we are caught up in it before we have time to consider its meaning.

But the presences which Brontë calls up are not merely persons. The whole physical scene, air and sky, house, dogs, furniture—all take on a life of their own. The traces of the past are inscribed on the present: names are flashed as if on a screen and implanted on our minds before we know to whom they refer—'a glare of white letters started from the dark as vivid as spectres—the air swarmed with Catherines'.

Thus, though the novel begins at a point when the action has almost run its course, the facts and contradictions which face us are not, as in a detective story, inert riddles to be solved by detached investigation. Mrs. Dean's brief, matter-of-fact answers to Lockwood's questions about family relationships tell him nothing. A series of shocks has assaulted his mind and body, and his interest in the history of Mr. Heathcliff has become a 'tiresomely active one', requiring a full, circumstantial narrative. The kind of curiosity which Brontë arouses demands a complete imaginative re-living of the past.

That is perhaps why the apparently artificial narrative structure she employs is necessary and convincing, and we are able to accept its conventions without question. Past and present interact on one another, forming a single, close-knit drama without division into Parts.

3. Nelly as Narrator

Though copious and detailed, Nelly's narrative has an extraordinary, sometimes breathless, energy, as if she were describing events that she had witnessed an hour ago, every moment of which is vividly present

[1] *The Disappearance of God*, 1963.

to her. In this art of stark immediacy—of making the past live for us in the present—we feel that the narrative is moulded by the pressure of events, and not that the shape and interpretation of events is being fashioned by the narrator. The sense of actuality is conveyed by a succession of precise concrete details that fall artlessly into place; and her sureness of touch seems to arise out of an astonishingly clear memory, especially for physical sensations. The impression of rapid excitement is achieved by concentrating our attention on movement and gesture, action and re-action, intermixed with vehement dialogue which convinces by its emphatic speech rhythms and plainness of language:

'Oh, if I were but in my own bed in the old house!' she went on bitterly, wringing her hands, 'And that wind sounding in the firs by the lattice. Do let me feel it!—it comes straight down the moor—do let me have one breath!'

To pacify her, I held the casement ajar a few seconds. A cold blast rushed through; I closed it, and returned to my post. She lay still now, her face bathed in tears. Exhaustion of body had entirely subdued her spirit; our fiery Catherine was no better than a wailing child.

There is no trace here of the conscious stylist. Catherine's words (with their sudden reminder of Lockwood's nightmare) seem to answer perfectly to Wordsworth's conception of poetry distilled to its bare essence—intense feeling overflowing in a naïve directness of language. The words 'it comes straight down the moor' might come from a good ballad or folk-song. (Consider what a difference it would make if we added the word 'from' after 'down', or if 'the' were substituted for the colloquial 'that' in the previous sentence.)

Notice too the brief rapidity of the sentences in the second paragraph; the way the sensation of cold is rendered by the active verb 'rushed'; and the absence of sentimentality in Nelly's diagnosis of Catherine's condition. The servant's familiar contempt for her mistress's childish tantrums is tempered by only a touch of motherly concern for her physical illness.

Nelly's value as a narrator is clear from this example. She brings us very close to the action and is, in one way, deeply engaged in it: the intimate affairs of the Heights and the Grange have taken up her whole life. Yet her air of righteous superiority towards Catherine and Heathcliff, her proprietary attitude towards those whom she has nursed as children, prevents her from being too emotionally involved in their affairs. As a professional housekeeper and natural busybody, her concern in events is chiefly a practical one, and she represents for us the commonsense point of view. (Suppose that one had to rewrite *Sense and Sensibility* from the point of view of Marianne Dashwood's housekeeper-companion: would she take a harsher view of Marianne than Jane Austen does?) Since Nelly always feels herself called upon to act responsibly, in the best interests (as she imagines) of her master and mistress, she has little time for the luxury of personal feeling.

Though decided in her views, Nelly is sometimes swayed hither and thither by pressures too powerful for her to understand, still less to control, and her own part in them is such as to make the reader doubtful of her judgements. Few readers today can accept her, as Charlotte Brontë did, as a 'specimen of true benevolence and homely fidelity'.[1] Her conventional religious and moral sentiments remind us of normal standards of behaviour, and at the same time are used ironically to stress the inadequacy of those standards and the moral blindness to which they can lead. One of the chief ways in which Brontë controls our responses, is by allowing us to feel we are more perceptive and imaginative than her narrators.

3. *Metamorphoses*

1. *A Gift from God* (*IV-V*)

The first part of Nelly's story lies far back in the perspective of time, taking us rapidly over a period of five years, with long gaps: a chiaroscuro picture, clearly focussed wherever the light falls, and leading us swiftly towards the second major close-up (after Catherine's diary), Heathcliff's narrative in VI.

Mr. Earnshaw's journey to Liverpool has something of the quality of biblical history (beginning, like Abraham's, early in the morning and lasting three days). His fateful action, like that of Lear and Leontes, appears largely unmotivated. Yet his emotional involvement is made apparent. Heathcliff is a substitute for a son that died in childhood. Mr. Earnshaw has struggled much ('flighted to death') to bring the waif

[1] Preface to her edition of *Wuthering Heights*, 1850.

home. 'You must e'en take it as a gift of God; though it's as dark almost as if it came from the devil'—his statement, like the witches' 'Fair is foul and foul is fair' in *Macbeth*, is mysteriously prophetic.

The waif is at first subhuman, a speechless 'it'. But on Nelly's return he is named, he is a 'he', he is 'thick' with Catherine and he can speak— a Caliban to whom she has taught language. The first words we hear from him are significant—the blunt assertion of dogged will, the Heath- cliff imperative that we hear again and again later: 'You must exchange horses with me: I don't like mine.' It is essential to register the full implications of this first highlighted incident, and the full extent to which Heathcliff has already been hardened and brutalised. The ragged creature that Earnshaw has placed before his family is an image of human nature reduced to its bare, animal essence, the naked will to live. What is said concerning Heathcliff's insensitiveness to pain and human feeling must be taken literally.

Chapter V gives us in swift succession the consequences of Earnshaw's folly and physical decay: Heathcliff's will to dominance fed by Earn- shaw's favouritism, and the growing ascendancy of Joseph over his master. Joseph and Heathcliff are both usurpers, thriving in the Heights on the Earnshaws' decline. Joseph encourages Earnshaw to 'regard Hindley as a reprobate', and as he takes control of the children's religious education, Catherine grows into 'a wild, wicked slip'. Immediately after Mr. Earnshaw's death, the future pattern is established: Catherine and Heathcliff are already, in fantasy, creating their private 'heaven' in terms that, as Nelly says with unconscious irony, 'no parson in the world' could ever imagine.

The death of Earnshaw[1] marks the beginning of the break-up of the traditional way of life at the Heights.

2. Displacements (VI)

The process of disintegration rapidly increases. Hindley's bringing his wife home at once destroys the community of the family sitting-room which was portrayed for us in the scene of Mr. Earnshaw's death. A foreign element of vulgar snobbery is introduced into the primitive household. Hindley's 'idolatry' towards his wife makes inevitable the tyranny which is, in effect, a complete loss of control; and Joseph's

[1] It is instructive to compare this with any of the well-known death-bed scenes in Dickens.

bibliocracy thrives on disorder, since 'it was his vocation to be where he had plenty of wickedness to reprove'. Thus, at a single step, we reach the explosive situation which has already been shown in Catherine's diary.

Heathcliff's narrative is clearly the sequel to that diary, continuing the story of the same Sunday. It is also complementary to it—the two together being a double mirror of the life that Heathcliff and Catherine had in common.

Though in part Heathcliff reflects Catherine's attitudes, his tone is very different from hers. There is nothing child-like here; Heathcliff never has been a child. Compared with her love, his is fixed, conscious, articulate: he is able at once to measure the spiritless Linton children against her 'immeasurable superiority', his own wild happiness against their pampered luxury. Catherine is wayward, a creature of childish extremes, living only in the moment; Heathcliff's immense will and shrewd intelligence is already set in one direction. The only counter-rhythms in his speech are those of hate and destruction.

We may notice first the redundant energy, assertiveness and crude force of his language. Like Caliban, he has profited from his education in that he knows how to curse. The strength and violence of his imagery arises from the sheer animal vigour of his feelings and perceptions: 'shrieking as if witches were running red-hot needles into her'; 'flinging Joseph off the highest gable, and painting the house-front with Hindley's blood'; 'as if she had been spitted on the horns of a mad cow'; 'shattering their great glass pane to a million fragments'.

Catherine's style is luminous, lyrical, charged with personal feeling: Heathcliff's is graphic, almost dehumanised, full of sensory detail (the bulldog's 'huge, purple tongue'); the ruthlessness of his contempt and pride, and his untameable energy, roar like a torrent over every incident he describes. The ghoulish insistency of his later speeches to Nelly is already latent here, but as yet it is not oppressive: the atmosphere is still vibrant with an abounding love of life transfigured for him by his love for Catherine.

The wild children from the Heights look in through the window from the stormy night without, and the luxury they glimpse appears at first like the 'heaven' of their childhood fantasy. But Heathcliff grasps at once the significance of the action going on there ('to quarrel who should hold a heap of warm hair'); he soon recoils, and his attitude to this 'heaven' of the civilised Lintons is determined for life. Catherine, on the other hand, being drawn inside and separated from Heathcliff, is at once bewitched by the dream. As Dorothy Van Ghent has put it:[1] 'She is taken in by the Lintons, and now it is Heathcliff alone outside looking through the window. . . . Thus the first snare is laid by which Catherine will be held for a human destiny—her feet washed, cakes and wine for her delectation, her beautiful hair combed (the motifs here are limpid as those of fairytale, where the changeling in the "otherworld" is held there mysteriously by bathing and by the strange new food he has been given to eat).'

But we do not need to invoke fairytale to see the effect in Brontë's narrative of these repeated displacements or sudden metamorphoses— the presents from Liverpool turned into the gibbering waif; Mr. Earnshaw asleep in his armchair, suddenly dead; Hindley returning an altered man, no longer an Earnshaw; the sweet, engaging Frances turning into a peevish, petted tyrant; and now, Catherine changed into a great lady. Every change brings a further threat to the innocence and integrity of childhood and of the Heights. The story moves through a series of vanishing perspectives; whenever Catherine or Heathcliff project their dream of happiness on to any concrete situation, they find it is not what they thought. The effect is to drive Catherine further from reality, and Heathcliff further outside the pale of the only human family to which he might have belonged.

4. Disintegration

1. From Fairytale to Inferno (VII)

In VII-IX Nelly's story covers a period of six years, though what we are in fact given is largely a dramatic close-up of two particular days, separated by the dialogue with Lockwood and the brief, lightly sketched story of the birth of Hareton and death of Frances. This break marks the watershed in the early part of the history: from here on, all that is left of the Earnshaw way of life disintegrates, and with it the childhood friendship of Catherine and Heathcliff.

In VII we have the only fully articulated picture of domestic life at

[1] *The English Novel, Form and Function* (Harper Torchbooks).

the Heights. But the old, cheerful way of life kept up by Nelly's Christmas preparations (and her striving to fit Heathcliff into the idyll) is poised on the edge of collapse. We are reminded here of the kind of house 'Wuthering Heights' once was,[1] linked with church, village and local traditions of carol singing, glees and dances. Joseph has no place in this 'devil's psalmody', and Heathcliff is forcibly excluded.

Thus the human drama that takes place exposes the unreality of these survivals. The superb scene of Catherine's return from the Grange dressed like a great lady dramatises in terms of cleanliness and touch the incompatibility between the Linton way of life and the raw simplicity of the Heights, whose life is still that of a farm. Heathcliff, like D. H. Lawrence's 'Blind Man', belongs to a world of dark stables. He here commands our sympathy, as much as any child of legend or literature who, being awake to the only generous feeling he has ever known, ('The notion of envying Catherine was incomprehensible to him') is driven to disgrace himself then abandoned to his misery.

The superficiality of Catherine's new social relationships, in contrast to the depth of her love for Heathcliff, is dramatised perfectly in the concrete details of the Christmas dinner, and her uncontrollable gush of tears. Her relationship with him is now like that of a princess in love with a prisoner in a dungeon.

Heathcliff's nature is never far from savagery, and now he is driven back to it: planning revenge is his only way of escape from misery— 'While I'm thinking of that I don't feel pain.' Here we have reached the source of the novel's main counter-theme, a ruthless, long-premeditated revenge gradually increasing in scope, with all the force of Heathcliff's primitive, unchanging will and shrewdness behind it. Nelly's fairytale 'prince in disguise' is destined to become a demon, taking on in fact the fiendishness she had seen lurking in his eyes; and 'Wuthering Heights', with its scent of spices and mulled ale, will very soon be turned into an 'infernal house'.

2. *Vanity-love* (*VIII*)

A glimpse of the sunny hayfields in June when 'the last of the Earnshaw stock' is born, then the disintegration of the household is complete. Hindley descends into his own helpless form of blasphemy and despair;

[1] Cf. Lockwood's description in I of the 'ranks of immense pewter dishes'.

Joseph becomes bailiff and the Heights is virtually cut off from the outside world.

Then there is a pause in the narrative while we take our first objective look at the main protagonists: Catherine now 'queen of the country-side' and 'full of ambition', yet forced to 'adopt a double character' since her life is rooted in her childhood at the Heights, still embodied for her in Heathcliff; Edgar, whose unchanging nature is placed before us once and for all in the fixed portrait; and Heathcliff, sinking back into the unregenerate state from which Catherine had reclaimed him—he recoils in shame from Catherine's 'girlish caresses',[1] and is no longer able to express his love.

Nelly's stocktakings are shrewd; they give us our bearings from the point of view of ordinary social and moral values. But they are never completely static: they describe a development and indicate a passage of time. In this, Brontë is closer to the D. H. Lawrence of The Rainbow[2] than to her fellow Victorians. For both Brontë and Lawrence show us how, for those (like Catherine Earnshaw or Anna and Ursula Brangwen) who are alive to its forces, life is always a process of change. Even Heathcliff's suspension of energy is shown here as a form of action, leading him inexorably in a certain direction. And in spite of Nelly's attempts to pin them down with adjectives, neither Catherine nor Cathy ever emerge as fully-formed 'characters'. As Derek Stanford has put it,[3] their most typical actions are 'those they perform once only. . . . They cannot be repeated, since fate has moved forward with their single performance.'

This is especially true of the mounting dramatic sequence of VIII-IX. All the incidents of the day of Heathcliff's disappearance interact to bring about the catastrophe. Their effect is to transform Catherine in our eyes from a wilful child ('she was not artful, never played the coquette') into a tragic heroine. Pulled between irreconcilable impulses, she is forced towards articulation and decision. In poetic utterance she now establishes her supremacy—but this cannot affect the course of events she has already set in motion. So her inner and outer lives are torn apart.

First, Catherine's conflict is presented objectively in terms of violent

[1] Is it, perhaps, because she is so girlish that she fails to educate him?
[2] I am thinking particularly of Lawrence's treatment of the childhood of both Anna and Ursula Brangwen.
[3] Op. cit.

action. Her two rival lovers seek her company at the same time, and 'the contrast resembled what you see in exchanging a bleak, hilly, coal country for a fertile valley'. It is a conflict between appearance and reality—the compulsive social pressure of vanity-love struggling against a suppressed weight of passion which offers no visible satisfaction. Her inward constancy gives way as she reduces Heathcliff to the dumb nonentity he was when Mr. Earnshaw first brought him home—'You might be dumb, or a baby, for anything you say to amuse me. . . .'

Her suppressed feeling of self-betrayal then vents itself on Nelly, because Nelly stands like her own conscience in the way of her vanity. To appease this vanity, she must exercise her power and have a victim. So she lures Edgar back and they confess themselves lovers. There is little here calculated to enlist our sympathy for Catherine.

3. The Storm Breaks (IX)

The inward struggle that takes place in the pauses of silence is amplified and distorted by the alternating scenes of chaotic violence. In the environment of Hindley's degeneracy, which we are forced to savour in the cut red herrings on the carving knife, Catherine must fight her battles alone. Hindley's running amok, like Joseph's grotesque comminations in moments of crisis, provides a cacophonous counterpoint to the real, gathering storm. Nelly knows that Hindley's violence is unreal. The language of his curses and sadistic violence ('flaying alive') seems a crude parody of the muscular energy which we noticed in Heathcliff's narrative. Yet by a bitter irony, this anti-masque which thrives on Heathcliff's inaction involves him in an action that precipitates his descent into brutality.

After the babel of shouts, squalls and kicks there follows an intense hush as Nelly sings her strange lullaby, with its reminder of Hareton's mother in the grave—'The mither beneath the mools (mould).'[1] We are conscious of Heathcliff's presence, as he lies brooding over the double frustration of the afternoon, when Catherine, unaware of him, breathlessly begins to tell Nelly her secret.

This long dialogue, its supple rhythms and counter-rhythms gathering momentum up to the great climax of 'Nelly, I *am* Heathcliff', expresses precisely the ebb and flow, the currents and undercurrents of Catherine's

[1] From a ballad 'The Ghaist's Warning'. See the Notes to Scott's *Lady of the Lake*, Canto IV, st XII, Note VI.

feeling. Nelly's impassivity, her harsh catechising, her attempt to escape, all lure Catherine on, forcing her to become increasingly articulate in order to evoke the response she needs. Nelly's is the language of common sense, Catherine's that of irrational feeling. There is a struggle for ascendancy between servant and mistress, commonplace wisdom striving in vain to overcome a gathering torrent. Catherine's urgent need to understand herself obliges her to seek in Nelly for some echo to reassure her, and reconcile the comparatively trivial 'secret' of her promise to marry Edgar with the deeper secret of her life's inner vision.

We can distinguish three stages in this struggle. The first is a quick to and fro between Catherine's girlish commonplaces about Edgar and Nelly's sharp, crusty comments. Since she is impervious to irony, Catherine finds no resistance in Nelly's answers and is maddened by her complacency: 'All seems smooth and easy: where is the obstacle?' Thus her sudden violent gesture and the compulsion to explain the nature of the obstacle. In this, the second stage, where she tries to give 'a feeling of how she feels' by telling her dream, she meets in Nelly a new layer of resistance, that of sincere dread and superstition. This obliges her to condense her dream to its bare essentials.

So in four swift clauses, perfect in their unconscious balance, alliteration, assonance and rhythm, she suddenly distils her life's most poignant experience. The dream is the source of a current of feeling that now flows into and shapes her language, reconciling contradictions and establishing connections which she cannot analyse, but only express in the emphatic movement of her speech and the assured finality of its imagery—'Whatever our souls are made of, his and mine are the same; and Linton's is as different as a moonbeam from lightning, or frost from fire.'

The flow is interrupted by Nelly's starting on seeing Heathcliff stealing out. Employing a tragic irony here, Brontë allows Catherine to fall back into self-deception. This at last draws Nelly out into the open: she speaks feelingly in defence of Heathcliff, confronting Catherine with the truth: 'As soon as you become Mrs. Linton, he loses friend, and love, and all!' Catherine is at once shocked (this is the third stage) into violent protest. There is no hesitation in her tone of voice now. Though her plan for using Edgar as a means of raising Heathcliff may have occurred to her on the spur of the moment, it has its own naïve kind of conviction; for Catherine strides over the mundane realities of marriage and money, thrusts aside Nelly's practical objection,

and suddenly breaks loose on a level of discourse which transcends the
conflict of human interests. The rhythm and language of her speech
reflect a personal apprehension of life that is 'carried alive into the heart
by passion'.[1] Misplace one accent, take away or transpose a single phrase,
and the words lose their resonance. There is, incredibly, no feeling of
strain in Catherine's placing the outcast Heathcliff in this cosmic setting
and so bringing together the extremes of personal and universal.

If further analysis is needed, notice the use of parallelism and repetition, especially the subtle alternation of pronouns and possessive adjectives, leading us by way of 'you/everybody/yours' to 'I/my/Heath-
cliff's' and so on to the emphatic 'If all else perished, and *he* remained, *I*
should still continue to be', followed by the transposition which can
now introduce 'the universe' quite naturally into the pattern; and the way
this rhythmic dance of personal pronouns is combined with abstract
words like 'existence', 'creation' and 'universe' so that these acquire the
ring of personal experience. Thus, after we have been carried through this
complex pattern of inter-relations, the final assertion of *identity* with
Heathcliff seems inevitable.

From a moral and prudential point of view, Catherine is childishly in
the wrong; yet the effect of this dialogue is to place her outside the
sphere of moral and social categories. Nelly's moralistic reply now
sounds just peevish and stupid. We guessed, as we read the words 'If all
else perished . . .', that Heathcliff had gone, and the universe had already
turned, for her, 'to a mighty stranger'. So the storm that comes 'rattling
over the Heights in full fury' drenching her to the skin—together with
the absurd croaking of Joseph, the scoldings of Nelly and the hectorings
of Hindley—are all part of the same cosmic polyphony. It is Catherine's
destiny, like Lear's, to have aroused these voices 'to parallel or contrary
motion'.[2]

Catherine's re-emergence from illness as a fixed character, overscored
with Nelly's moral judgements, leaves the reader detached and disengaged, since the drama is now suspended. Catherine without Heathcliff is a mere shell, and the contours of the story here fall away steeply
so that the three years leading to her marriage with Edgar are scarcely
visible. The 'real' Catherine only begins to re-emerge and undergo
further development when Heathcliff returns.

[1] Wordsworth, Preface to *Lyrical Ballads*.
[2] Auerbach, op. cit., XIII.

5. A Hell in Heaven's Despite

1. The Hero turned Wolf (X)

Hitherto the action has centred on the Heights and we have seen its life only from within. With Nelly's move to the Grange, the direction of our vision changes: the sequestered realm of civilised life is now in the foreground, Heathcliff and the Heights are sinister threats beyond the pale. As the Grange holds Catherine in a kind of enchantment, so it casts a spell on the reader; thus our sympathies now become more perplexed.

The new mood is established by images of sweetness and reflected moonlight (Edgar's soul has been compared to a moonbeam). Into this deathly stillness, Heathcliff's reappearance as a dark form lurking amidst shadows brings life, movement, intense excitement. The narrative moves indoors, and in a swift sequence of scenes we witness a domestic idyll turned by this incursion into a drama of conflict and brutality, leading finally to frenzy.

It begins in the alert manner of domestic comedy, Heathcliff's entry revealing the flaws beneath the polished surface of a form of life that has no place for displays of spontaneous feeling. (Edgar's indulgence is a concession to *sentiment*.) Then, as Catherine's excitement drives her to confide in Nelly, the narrative plunges into the flux of her contradictory feelings: trying to keep a grip on social obligations, but already losing it. The interaction of these planes of reality disengages our moral and social sympathies, as the action grows more complex, by imposing on them too great a strain: so we are obliged to witness the drama as an inevitable conflict of supra- or subhuman forces.

We do not *recognise* Heathcliff as a returned romantic hero. As in reading a play like *Macbeth*, we must 'trust the tale' and not force ourselves to connect different parts of the story when the effect is to dislocate our sympathies. The picture of Heathcliff is not built up by a continuous process of character development, but by stratified layers of association which are not all equally present at the same time. In this, Brontë's method is closer to that of poetic drama than the novel of 'character'.

Heathcliff's presence awakens all the latent passions in others. In trying to convince Isabella's romantic innocence of the reality of the inhuman, Catherine defines his nature in terms of brutish forces outside human sympathy: 'a fierce, pitiless, wolfish man'. This is reinforced by the glimpse of the sordid horror going on at the Heights which we get from Nelly, who superimposes Joseph's wry, threatening voice on to the drawing-room dialogue.

But the scene of cold, offhand brutality which follows in the library lacks even the poetry of unreclaimed nature; it reveals Heathcliff's inhumanity in a more repulsive light. Heathcliff and Catherine look on Isabella as animals regard a 'strange, repulsive' creature; the action is all scratching, clawing, clutching, wrenching, the language that of beasts of prey. Isabella herself is brutalised, all human feeling is excluded.

2. The Wolf turned Demon (XI)

In XI the narrative plunges again, to reveal the source of one of its main elements, Nelly's own superstitious dread. Her ecstatic experience of return to childhood, followed by loss, yearning and superstitious fear, is related with the terse, graphic precision of a folk tale. It reveals how even a woman as sober as she could come to regard one of her foster-children as an incarnate goblin. The convincing metamorphoses here (turning the visionary child Hindley into the elf-locked Hareton, who is himself transformed) give us a powerful impression of Heathcliff as a source of uncanny evil, able to turn the innocence of childhood to devilry.

This prepares us for the greater changes which Catherine now has to face—which will lead her, in the end, to deny that this Heathcliff *is* the one she loves in her soul.

Nelly's narrative carries us in brief, detached sentences, through a tense, swift scene of angry dialogue and physical conflict, to the breaking-point where Catherine loses all control of those around her: 'She rang the bell till it broke with a twang . . .' A plain, three-cornered kitchen conflict becomes a drama of her soul, governed by Brontë's own psycho-dynamic laws.

We are not concerned here with characters, like Jane Eyre for example, who struggle resolutely to come to terms with life as it is, or whose speech is always 'sincere'.[1] Brontë's characters are not reflective; their

[1] Cf. Nelly's comment on Catherine's attempt to use her frenzy as a means of frightening Edgar: 'for they [Catherine's instructions] were

words partake of the nature of actions and their actions are the direct enacting of inner conflicts. Catherine's egoism consists in her completely identifying the outer world with herself. Edgar *is* her pride, security and tranquillity ('Quarrel with Edgar . . . and you'll hit on exactly the most efficient method of revenging yourself on *me*'); Heathcliff *is* the wild, free life of her childhood which she cannot give up: thus she must keep both. If either of them change, or cease to conform, her life falls apart.

Before Edgar's intervention, Catherine has become aware of a transformation in Heathcliff. His speech has acquired a new hammer-blow rhythm as his impulse to revenge now turns directly against Catherine herself—'What new phase in his character is this?' She sees beneath his unreclaimed nature something of his diabolism, and a direct connection is now established with the child who vowed revenge against Hindley: 'It is as bad as offering Satan a lost soul. Your bliss lies, like his, in inflicting misery.'

This change in Heathcliff releases a destructive energy in Catherine ('The spirit which served her was growing intractable') and Edgar is now the scapegoat. She clings more tenaciously to Heathcliff through her instinct for self-identification. The action, which pivots on the locked inner door and her flinging the key on the fire, represents the escape from her grasp of both men on whom her sanity depends. By trapping Edgar she reduces him to nullity ('a sucking leveret'), and provokes him to the act of desperate defiance which enables him to escape. Then the same lock becomes a trap for Heathcliff and she is obliged to let him smash his way out. In losing control of the one, she has lost control of the other.

So the wild, unformed energy in Catherine spends itself in a paroxysm of rage. With her failure to force Edgar into submission she loses her last hold on the present and sinks into the deeper delirium which is, in fact, a delayed reaction to her life's deeper loss—'I was a child . . . and my misery arose from the separation that Hindley had ordered between me and Heathcliff. I was laid alone for the first time. . . .' (XII)

delivered in perfect *sincerity*; but I believed a person who could plan the turning of her fits of passion to account, beforehand, might, by exerting her will, manage to control herself tolerably. . . .' The irony here is that Catherine *is* sincere, in her own way: she could *not* manage to control herself if she failed to control Edgar. All her words inevitably express the need to force her will on others.

3. The Lost Heaven (XII)

All the dammed-up currents of Catherine's being now change direction and flow backward—away from Edgar, through the traumatic experience of childhood and on towards death, which she now sees as the only way to regain her lost heaven 'in the middle of the moor'.

This passage of Catherine's delirium distils the poetry which gives meaning to her history. Every reader must trace for himself the delicate shifts of time and mood as her mind, rising and sinking, refracts and illuminates, in reverie and waking dream, elements that we remember from earlier parts of the story—the oak closet and black clothes press, the wind sounding in the firs by the lattice, the graves in Gimmerton Kirk. Hers is a child's world of separate images, a language of symbolism and suggestion. Untrammelled by worldly realities, her mind reshapes and creates new images which startle us with a strange truth of their own (Nelly as an old witch 'gathering elf-bolts to hurt us'); and the rhythm of her bare language is memorable like that of great legends or myths: 'It's a rough journey, and a sad heart to travel it; and we must pass by Gimmerton Kirk, to go that journey.'

But this is highly organised *dramatic* poetry, triumphing again over Nelly's common sense as much through gesture and action as words. Consider, for example, her ranging the feathers on the sheet.

First of all the lapwing is free, wheeling in the sky. With the struggle to get back to its nest, the rhythm becomes heavier. There is a pause. Catherine falters, and we are aware only of the single feather in her hand. The broken narrative now moves on haltingly, seeming to contradict itself. The lapwing, like Catherine herself, can never get back to its nest on the heath: Heathcliff's wanton cruelty has set a snare over it. She tried to control him, making him promise never to shoot another lapwing—but there are more lapwing feathers on the pillow: 'Did he shoot my lapwings, Nelly? Are they red, any of them?' The questions have a terrible urgency for Catherine. What has Heathcliff done? Has he betrayed her? What has happened to that heaven on the moor which he once shared?

Like Ophelia's madness and Lady Macbeth's sleep-walking, Catherine's delirious speech is held in place by the total dramatic situation of which it forms a part—the disruption of Thrushcross Grange by Heathcliff. The main plot is kept moving, striding over Catherine's flickering half-life and forcing us to question what her vision has to do with the Heathcliff who is now prime mover in the action.

The melodrama of Isabella's elopement is deliberately rendered trivial by the yelping of the little dog and the careless indifference of village gossip. In their useless fluster about Catherine, both Edgar and Nelly relinquish Heathcliff's first human victim without a murmur. Heathcliff's hatred and Catherine's brain fever have exposed the heartlessness that underlies the luxury of the Grange. Catherine pictures Edgar, after her death, 'offering prayers of thanks to God for restoring peace to his house, and going back to his books!' Heathcliff shows us Isabella content to abandon her brother and allow her favourite dog to be hanged for an illusion of romance. We begin to see a savage, Swiftian satire in his actions. Catherine's yearning for an unearthly beauty, Heathcliff's pursuit of ugliness for its own sake—together form a dialectic which is beginning to strip the mask off civilisation.

6. A Moral Teething

Brontë allows us little pause for breath: in a series of ever changing encounters, each conflict moves on to its climax. In these chapters the Heights appears to overwhelm the Grange; Heathcliff assumes his full stature, and the strident theme of his revenge for a while silences the fragile theme of Catherine's mystical longing. But in the great death-struggle of XV this theme asserts its strength, and in her passing into death Catherine seems to triumph over Heathcliff. Then in XVI and XVII his will takes command more powerfully than before, and he completes his revenge on Hindley. Avarice seems to take the place of love; he lives on in a spiritual void—'sinking in the endless undoing, the awful katabolism into the abyss'[1]—while Catherine has apparently passed beyond the orbit in which she was held to Heathcliff.

1. Re-entering the Penetralium (XIII-XIV)

By means of Isabella's letter we now re-enter the Heights, seeing it afresh with extraordinary vividness through her wondering eyes. Serving

[1] D. H. Lawrence, *The Hands of God* (*Last Poems*).

a similar function to that of the two opening chapters of Lockwood's diary, the grotesque observations and ironies of the letter provide a prelude to what follows.

Isabella's description gives us another microcosm, and illustrates a further stage in the process of change. The present chaos, shown in the picturesque details of decay and desolation, stands midway between the old order of the Earnshaws and the new one to be imposed by Heathcliff as landlord.[1] If the novel did not give us this physical and social history of a real household, some of its main events might seem as fanciful as those of a romantic drama like *The Cenci*.

We should also note the startling changes wrought in Isabella, the proofs of Heathcliff's power (her touching Hindley's two-edged weapon, and finding her own mood mirrored in his eyes); and the way Joseph's comic resistance to invasion divides our sympathies, so that we are drawn into an irrational siding with the inmates of the Heights, such as we may feel in *Gulliver* for the Yahoos.

In XIV we at last meet Heathcliff face to face, in a way that we have never done since his narrative in VI. Coming to terms with what he is demands of the reader an honesty which only Dostoevsky, among other novelists, has the power to enforce.

Heathcliff's effect on others is to strip them of all the trappings of personality except passion. A man whose deepest desires have been thwarted is driven to extort from others a passionate response at any price. His sadism is a substitute for love: violence is necessary because Brontë's aim is to show us this particular 'hell'.

Hypersensitive about all that concerns Catherine, Heathcliff is provoked by Nelly's insensitivity into a torrential harangue—'forcing himself to seem calm'. The power of his insistent speech derives from a cruel logic hammered home by parallelism and repetition. The violent images and hyperboles express an impetuous will that cannot brook opposition, and his rhetoric hardens, as it gathers momentum, into a language of absolute imperatives.

His words shock and fascinate by their appalling honesty; and in this he may, perhaps, be compared to his anti-type in fiction, Dostoevsky's Christ-like Myshkin.[2] His logic depends on a refusal to admit any

---

[1] Cf. XVIII: 'but the house, inside, had regained its ancient aspect of comfort . . .', etc.

[2] The only 'characters' in fiction who at all resemble Heathcliff are

compromise with passion, any form of mediocrity. Given his assumptions, his rhetorical questions would seem conclusive and his conclusions absolute (e.g. 'How can she love in him what he has not?') Thus the force of his language lies not so much in any positive values it creates, as in its savage, destructive satire.

In his muttered 'I have no pity!...', etc., his thoughts move forward by both logic and a transferred association of images, with a cryptic, Shakespearean effect. The crushing of worms suggests to him the grinding of teeth, this in turn a teething baby. Now he takes up the application for *him* of teething: it is 'a moral teething', that is, a growing up into a new morality of his own (using Isabella to cut the teeth of his revenge and outgrow all feelings of pity and humanity).[1] Teething suggests to him pain for the one who grinds, but his imagination transposes the idea of pain back to the crushed worms and thus restores the image to its original purpose.

Being deprived of his own humanity, he cannot bear that others should show human qualities. He habitually refers to human beings in terms of animal life, and recoils from any display of tender feeling as from a snake-bite.[2]

2. The Demon let Loose (XV-XVII)

Heathcliff's sudden bursting into Catherine's reverie by the open lattice is one of the boldest, most dramatic moments in the novel. Yet Brontë's astonishing achievement in this scene is largely one of sheer logic: she simply follows the dialectic of Heathcliff's and Catherine's contradictory passions to their conclusion, presenting them fearlessly in all their inhuman intensity. Nelly describes their words and movements baldly, with detachment, as one might describe the ferocious struggle of two caged wild beasts. The effect is of two beings successively flung together and torn apart—heaving, held asunder, springing, catching, locked, gripping, clasping. All these verbs of muscular movement and the adjectives describing bodily and facial expressions (burning,

Dostoevsky's Satanic heroes (Svidrigailov, Stavrogin, etc.) and Melville's Captain Ahab.

[1] Notice how the image of teeth keeps recurring in Isabella's narrative (XVII).

[2] Cf. his disgust at Cathy's kisses in XXI, or his reaction to her pleading in XVII: ' "Keep your eft's fingers off; and move, or I'll kick you!" cried Heathcliff, brutally repulsing her.'

throbbing, livid, etc.) convey the idea of human beings involuntarily possessed by inhuman powers stronger than sexual love, and too consuming and unbearable for human flesh. In their speech, too, there is no playing upon tender feelings: they speak the truth to one another without deception, though they both know that Catherine is dying.

'The emotions of Heathcliff and Catherine', said E. M. Forster,[1] 'function differently to other emotions in fiction. Instead of inhabiting the characters, they surround them like thunder clouds, and generate the explosions that fill the novel.'

At the same time, Brontë is precise, and the thunder clouds have clear edges. It is essential for the reader to analyse each action and reaction and see exactly in what ways Heathcliff's and Catherine's passions of rage and anguish exceed their power to understand each other. The struggle centres on Catherine's believing that he will not follow her to the grave and 'brave its ghosts' as he did as a child, and his failure to comprehend her longing for death. This leads to her unexpected breaking away into the lyrical vision of her own 'glorious world' where the 'Heathcliff' within her soul is disassociated, at least momentarily, from the living, unforgiving Heathcliff. Yet in the final embrace which causes her death, she believes that he has at last responded to her appeal, so that her dead face 'asserts its own tranquillity'. Nelly too is then swept up in the current of Catherine's feeling, expressing an 'assurance' of the 'shadowless hereafter' in which we can recognise, for once, the voice of Brontë ('No coward soul is mine') speaking through her narrator.

But Heathcliff thinks Catherine has deceived him by dying in peace, so he invokes on her the curse of an unquiet grave. If we compare Heathcliff's terrible cry 'Oh God! it is unutterable! . . .', etc. with the words spoken by Marlowe's Faustus in his last moments,[2] Heathcliff's anguish may appear far from Promethean. His agony is more like that of a beast deprived of its prey—'being goaded to death by knives and spears'. He is punishing himself because his thirst for vengeance has so overrun his love for Catherine that she has escaped him and left him soulless.

Thus Heathcliff is left on earth a 'brute beast' or 'incarnate goblin', and Isabella's narrative in XVII, charged with electric hatred and

[1] *Aspects of the Novel*, VII.
[2] I am thinking particularly of the passage 'Why wert thou not a creature wanting soul? . . .', etc. where Faustus wishes he had been born a 'brutish beast'.

violence, is the dramatic amplification of his tortured agony in XVI. His destructive energy is released in a climacteric of blood-letting that corresponds, in its ugly way, to the release of passion in the frenzy that followed Catherine's paroxysm of rage.

The reader expects a respite, but no sooner is Catherine buried than the weather changes to a second winter, the delicate spring-like beauty which surrounds her death is blasted, and Isabella, shot out of the Heights like a bolt into the sleet and snow, carries all its savagery straight into the quiet parlour of the Grange, where the puny child Cathy is being nursed. All her romanticism has now been burned away by the 'purgatory' of the Heights, and her hysterical speech pours out in a torrent, as the water pours from her thin frock and the blood from her wound.

Isabella's story is filled with verbs of violent physical action which (as Dorothy Van Ghent has put it)[1] 'seethe with a brute fury' ('kicked and trampled on him, and dashed his head repeatedly on the flags'). It derives its force, too, from her intense personal vision of Heathcliff's demonic nature—his 'basilisk eyes' which are 'the clouded windows of hell', his 'sharp, cannibal teeth . . . gleaming through the dark', etc. Like the other inset narratives, it also gives a fuller significance to objects which we have already caught a glimpse of (the spring-knife which recoils on its owner, the narrow lattices whose stanchions Heathcliff now crashes through like a bull, etc.).

But the meaning here does not all lie on the surface. The motives of Heathcliff's actions (for example, his desperate eagerness to get back to his chamber) are not all clearly explained; and since the causes of the action are partly invisible, they cannot be fully understood in human terms. If we add to this the various connections with other parts of the narrative—for example, between Lockwood's rubbing the ghost-child's wrist on the broken pane and (though it belongs to a different order of reality) Heathcliff's slitting of Hindley's wrist, also at a broken pane— the total impression is of Heathcliff as thrall to primitive forces which he cannot control. Our minds connect these forces with the spirit of Catherine, to whom he prays 'till he grows hoarse and his voice is strangled in his throat'.

However, such shadowings are only passing and momentary. Outwardly, Isabella's narrative leads us straight to the completion of Heathcliff's revenge against Hindley and his becoming master of the Heights.

[1] Op. cit.

At the same time Edgar, nursing his Tennysonian grief, declines into nonentity by cutting himself off from the last vestiges of public life. So to all outward appearance, Heathcliff is victorious, the influence of the Grange is shrunk almost to nothing and the child Cathy seems already destined to become Heathcliff's next victim.

It is, therefore, significant that Heathcliff now 'rapidly regains flesh', and that this chapter should descend by stages from the language of violence to that of kinship, property-rights and wills. For the outcome of the struggle between the two houses is now only a matter of time, patience and legalistic guile; his love and hate appear to be running away into the shallow channels of avarice. Heathcliff the fiend is becoming Heathcliff the surly, tight-fisted landlord.

7. The Breeze-rocked Cradle

Chapters XVIII-XXXI form the slow movement in the novel's structure, where the deathward impulse of the action caused by the separation of Catherine and Heathcliff gradually paralyses the life of young Cathy, till the plot is brought to a standstill in XXX.

At first there is relief from tension. Nelly's narrative becomes more transparent in texture and more leisurely in movement. Since Cathy is brought up in the earthly paradise of the Park by Nelly, who constantly refers to her as 'angel' or 'fairy',[1] her life is one of make-believe and romance.

The drama now depends for its effect more on changes of mood and tone, and less on decisive action. The final confrontation between the two houses is repeatedly delayed, as Cathy, with no one but Nelly to guide her, struggles through a series of childish illusions. Heathcliff's features are hidden under a series of masks (landlord, uncle, match-maker and father); his presence is felt in the action only as a sinister face concealed in a child's puzzle-picture.[2] He never fully reveals his brutal

[1] 'She who was always "love," and "darling," and "queen," and "angel," with everybody at the Grange, to be insulted so shockingly by a stranger!' (XVIII).
[2] Note, for example, Heathcliff's stiff style evident in the letter (XXV) supposed to have been written by Linton.

nature to Cathy until he has her trapped in the Heights. Meanwhile the petty snares he lays for her slowly reduce her to powerlessness and passivity: her efforts to break loose into positive action are made futile; and finally her life is led into imprisonment and becomes a living death.

The story of Cathy derives a great deal of its meaning from its relationship to that of Catherine. Every incident which Nelly dwells on has to do with her struggle to come to terms with the Heights. Her dissatisfaction with her secluded Eden[1] leads her to leap over the Park fence and go in search for that world beyond which is represented for her by the Heights—and so she escapes from one closed world into another which proves a real prison. So Catherine's words about the 'shattered prison' from which she was 'wearying to escape' still dominate the action; and we may remark here how important the ideas of enclosure and escape, and the image of lock and key,[2] are in *Wuthering Heights*.

As Brontë creates her own logic of passion, so too she creates a convincing logic of heredity: the children of love, Cathy and Hareton, combine the positive qualities of both their parents; the child of hate, Linton, the negative ones. Thus Cathy is in part a reincarnation of Catherine, and her story gains significance through the parallels and contrasts by which it is related to that of her mother. In scenes of rain and storm, Catherine's spirit appears to have an independent existence among the elements. But in these calmer scenes of sunshine and shadow which now intervene, we feel Catherine's presence in the spirit of Cathy, whose moods are reflected in the landscape and weather, and whose face mirrors that of nature.[3] Her attraction has something of the elusive quality of Wordsworth's Lucy.[4]

1. Escaping to the Otherworld (XVIII–XXI)

As the luxuries of the Grange once tempted Catherine, so the magic of the Fairy Cave now tempts Cathy to her doom. Her story begins with the irrevocable action of her escaping into the 'otherworld' of the Heights. Her first meeting with Hareton is a little like the meeting of

---

[1] 'The Grange is not a prison, Ellen . . .' (XXIII).
[2] Cp. Cathy's struggle with Heathcliff for the key (XXVII), the incident at the locked Park door (XXII), and Catherine's flinging the key on the fire (XI).
[3] 'Catherine's face was just like the landcape—shadows and sunshine flitting over it in rapid succession . . .' (XXVII).
[4] Cf. the lyric 'Three years she grew in sun and shower.'

children in a fairytale—his 'canine followers' attacking Cathy's 'train'.
Heathcliff is absent—his existence barely hinted at in Hareton's promise
to show her 'where the goblin-hunter rises on the marsh'.

Yet this escape leads at once to the shock of Cathy's first encounter
with a harsher reality: Hareton changed into a cursing menial and then
foisted on her as 'cousin'. She is faced with a real problem of relationships
and social status affecting her view of the outside world. This leads her
to give away the secret of Linton's forthcoming arrival, which sets
Heathcliff's plot in motion.

Linton's arrival at the Grange (XIX) may be contrasted with the
earlier scenes (IV and IX) of Heathcliff's first arrival at the Heights
(Heathcliff rendered inhuman by ill-treatment, Linton by coddling),
and later at the Grange. Father and son represent two extremes of
selfishness which are ultimately seen to be akin, and Cathy's sympathy
for Linton's sufferings provides a shallow counterpart to Catherine's
sharing of Heathcliff's miseries. Here, as in X, the tea-table comedy
introduces a series of events which gradually turn from domestic
idyll to cruel conflict.

Like Joseph, Linton is an extreme example of a type of humanity that
borders on the grotesque, but he is made fully convincing in terms of
physique, speech and manners. Brontë also uses him as a vehicle of
parody, and a symbol (like a death's head fixed on the arm of a settle!)
of the life-denying characteristics in both families. He reflects Edgar's
weakness and Heathcliff's wilfulness, and perpetually reminds us of all
that is most debilitating in the Lintons' comfort as well as in Heathcliff's
restless self-torment.

Yet he is made to exercise an influence almost as powerful as that of
Conrad's dying 'nigger' over the crew of the *Narcissus*. His presence
causes Heathcliff, now deprived of any object of personal pride,[1] to
resort to petty intrigue, turning Linton into a sinister 'cockatrice' (the
counterpart to the fatal 'basilisk') in order to make a mockery of his
enemies. So, in his own way, Linton naturalises himself and becomes
another usurper at the Heights—rejecting its wholesome porridge, which
has nurtured Hareton, in favour of milk, and making its domestic life
more distorted.

In XXI, the drama by which Cathy is enmeshed, shown in a variety of

[1] 'If I wished for any blessing in the world, it was to find him a worthy
object of pride.' (XX)

incidents scattered over several years, gradually assumes the character of a life and death struggle. It begins with Cathy bounding up the Heights on a spring day, and ends with her listless and disillusioned. The fullness with which Nelly dwells on such small incidents as the discovery and burning of the letters stresses the childishness to which Heathcliff is reducing both Cathy and her nurse by taking advantage of their weaknesses.

2. The Death-trap (XXII-XXVIII)

Cathy and Linton are doomed to suffer for the sins of their parents; she is also the instrument by which the fates of both houses will be reversed. So a great deal depends on her reaction to every trivial incident of her life, which is accordingly magnified. To achieve this effect, Brontë makes nature, and particularly the weather and seasonal changes, influence the changes in the lives of Cathy and Linton. To him, fresh air is 'killing'; he cannot bear to have the window left open in the evening;[1] the 'salubrious' and 'genial' air of the Heights, which is life-giving to the strong but deadly to the weak and ailing,[2] does not (as Nelly hopes) prove healthier for him. It increases his listlessness.

But Cathy's 'sparkling spirit' is equally at home in the Park or on the Heights, whose air is only sullied for her by Heathcliff's presence there and the use he makes of Linton. And the 'clouding over' of Cathy's spirit is depicted in the interplay of weather and mood both in the valley and on the moor.

With the change in weather and the onset of Edgar's illness in XXII, the story grows more sombre and Cathy becomes 'starved and sackless'. Her loneliness and exposure are reflected in the image of the last bluebell under the trees where in summer she used to swing in ecstasy. Significantly, she is now exposed to Heathcliff's influence by being locked outside the Park gate and unable to scale its 'ramparts'. 'Catherine's heart', Nelly tells us, was now 'clouded over with double darkness.'

This meeting with Heathcliff leads her into the 'love-scene' of XIII, in which we see Linton in a 'fit' (screaming, writhing and working himself into a 'passion'). This may be read as a burlesque of earlier scenes between Catherine and Edgar or Heathcliff (e.g. VIII and XV).

[1] 'Oh! it's killing! a breath of night air! . . .', etc. (XXI)
[2] 'Every breath from the hills so full of life, that it seemed whoever respired it, though dying, might revive. . . .' (XXVII)

But at the same time, Linton truly 'racks' Cathy beyond endurance. Thus she is drawn more deeply into the trap Heathcliff has laid for her, which is not only to bring her to the forbidden house, but also to perplex her feelings and sense of duty by involving her in an affair in which she is powerless.

In the incidents of her own narrative[1] in XXIV, the conflict of her feelings is increased and intensified.[2] She experiences something of the violence of the Heights in Hareton's brutal rage and Linton's 'powerless fury'. At the same time, all that is positive in her childhood is summed up in the prose poem where she describes her 'perfect idea of heaven's happiness'. The verdant richness, the glancing light, the sound and movement of the fertile valley are enacted in the rhythm of her prose as vividly as her mother's childhood ecstasy was in that of her 'dream'. But Cathy's 'heaven' amidst the changing foliage of cultivated nature is very different from Catherine's, with its 'hardy, savage freedom'. It is more like the 'jubilee' of Wordsworth's *Immortality Ode*—the 'heaven' which 'lies about us in our infancy'.

But Cathy, at this stage, is a *spoilt* child of nature, and Brontë is careful to place her 'heaven' in a more realistic, and juvenile, context than Wordsworth, associating it with her childish love for Linton. In XXII, Nelly had mentioned the same 'rocking' action as Cathy describes here, and explicitly compared it to the motion of an infant's cradle: 'She would lie in her breeze-rocked cradle, doing nothing but singing old songs—my nursery lore—to herself, or watching the birds, joint tenants, feed and entice their young ones to fly. . . .' Her childhood happiness is a fragile interlude between Isabella's and her own imprisonment in the Heights. As for Linton's 'heaven', its deathly stillness[3] will very soon be realised: his lying 'on a bank of heath' will be the means of decoying Cathy into Heathcliff's 'hell'.

In XXV, the close, sultry weather of a summer already past its prime, like the clouded moonlight of Coleridge's *Christabel*, conveys an oppressive sense of deception and approaching doom. The last meetings on the moor between Cathy and the dying Linton are more monstrous, perhaps, than the novel's earlier scenes of *physical* violence, as these involve

[1] Cathy's story, with its petty rebellion against Nelly's authority, may be contrasted with that of her mother's diary in III.

[2] 'I wished to go exceedingly; but I was *strangely excited* . . .', etc. (XXIV)

[3] 'I said his heaven would be only half alive . . .', etc. (XXIII)

mental torture. Linton is stricken with terror at the prospect of Heathcliff's imminent arrival over 'a nab of heath', like the devil coming to carry off his prisoners.[1] It is worth noting that though Nelly's wits are paralysed, Cathy reacts with vigour and her contempt for Linton's cowardice reminds us of the way her mother might have spoken—'Rise, and don't degrade yourself into an abject reptile—*don't*!'

Once Cathy is safely shut up in the Heights, Heathcliff shows the same brutality as he did to Isabella eighteen years before. Nelly, too, meets with the punishment she deserves for her constant ambivalence— officially on the side of the Lintons, yet repeatedly serving Heathcliff's purposes. In XXVIII, Zillah's callousness towards Nelly, Heathcliff's pointless cruelty in preventing Cathy from returning to her father's bedside, and lastly, Linton's ugly narrative, confirm our impression of a household barren of all human feeling. The last remnants of Cathy's power of resistance seem to be destroyed now, as Heathcliff smashes her portrait of her father and deals her a crushing blow that makes her mouth bleed. Her fate is mysteriously linked with that of the dead by her escaping into the moonlit night of Edgar's death by the same lattice through which the ghost-child tries to enter.[2] She returns to the Grange only to witness its dispersal at the hands of Heathcliff's lawyer.

8. Married to Death

1. The Unquiet Grave (XXIX)

We have previously associated the Grange library with the Lintons' passivity; now Cathy and Nelly sit there when Heathcliff comes to collect them. By her three times repeating the words 'the same' ('the same room . . . the same moon . . . the same autumn landscape') Nelly stresses the futility of Heathcliff's triumph. He himself is as much the victim of a meaningless fate as they.

Yet Brontë chooses this moment to bring about a sudden stirring in the depths of Heathcliff's mind which obliges us to come to terms with him again; she achieves this by a brief interchange which recalls the past.

[1] 'You would imagine I was the devil himself, Miss Linton, to excite such horror. . . .' (XXVII)
[2] This escape may partly account for the soldered hasp in III.

Cathy, no longer under any illusions about Heathcliff, 'enters into the spirit of her future family': she speaks to him 'with a kind of dreary triumph', showing a new insight like her mother's—her words 'You *are* miserable, are you not? Lonely, like the devil . . .', etc. remind us of Catherine's 'It's as bad as offering Satan a lost soul . . .', etc. (XI). Heathcliff is moved, and drives Cathy out. Then he turns idly to Catherine's portrait. Perhaps it is a sense of the emptiness of his victory, suggested by the picture of which he has no need, which now leads him to boast to Nelly about the only real triumph he has striven for. Once started, he is carried away by his story till at the end 'his hair clung to his forehead, wet with perspiration'.

Here we have reached the heart of the novel and the key to the problems that surround its hero. He describes two visits to Catherine's grave, one at the beginning, the other ('yesterday') at the end of the eighteen years of his revenge. Thus they enclose and give new meaning to all that has happened since Catherine's death. As frequently happens in *Wuthering Heights*, their time sequence is reversed, so that we may interpret the past in the light of the present.[1]

The oppressive repetitions of his earlier, angry speeches (e.g. in XIV) and the heavy formality of his later, hypocritical ones (e.g. in XXII) here fall away. He speaks with the immediacy of powerful feeling in a language which, though still abrupt and vehement, conveys his experience directly, in terms of acute physical sensations (Catherine's 'warm breath . . . displacing the sleet-laden wind'). Every feeling he describes affects the nerves. There is no distinction for him between the physical and the spiritual, or between natural and supernatural. Beneath his callousness, there is a child-like capacity for elemental feeling, which reaches a terrible intensity when he describes his yearning to see Catherine once more.

With complete simplicity Heathcliff affirms again his 'strong faith in ghosts', as he did in XVI. His story makes clear the nature of that 'reality' of the Heights which Lockwood, though involved in it, was unable to grasp. It is the reality of ballad and folk-lore. Heathcliff's failure to develop as a convincing 'character' is due to the concentration of all his passion on one object, his relationship with the dead.[2]

The effect of both incidents is temporarily to divert him from thoughts

---

[1] Has Catherine disturbed Heathcliff's peace, or he hers?
[2] Cp. the effect on Macbeth of his visit to the witches.

of vengeance and to 'console' him. But the consequences are different in each case. Through the first (in order of time) his impulse to lie in the earth with Catherine had been turned into a sense of her presence *above* the earth, so palpable that he talked to her on his way back to the Heights and expected to find her in his chamber. With a shock we now recognise the night described in Isabella's story as the same, and re-interpret its violence. (Was it his shedding of Hindley's blood that caused his disenchantment, turning the spirit of Catherine into a tormentor, so that he was forced in the end to abandon the haunted room?[1] And could Lockwood's shedding of the revenant's blood in his 'nightmare' have inadvertently completed the cycle of revenge, so restoring to Heath-cliff the Catherine whose presence he lost when he grappled with Hindley at the broken lattice?)

His second visit to the grave has the reverse effect. Seeing her features preserved in the peat makes him realise again that she *is* dead and he can only return to her, as he originally intended, by sharing her sleep of death. So his longing to see her again is stilled and, intent on death, he gives his instructions to the sexton.[2] If we now place Lockwood's nightmare in the time-sequence (between XXX and XXXI) it is relevant to ask: What must have been the effect on Heathcliff of the revenant's renewed attempt to get in to him? And how does this affect our under-standing of the final chapters? For Lockwood's nightmare complements this narrative of Heathcliff's, and the two together, placed near the beginning and end of the story, form the deepest 'layer of association' by which we may understand 'the history of Mr. Heathcliff'.

Brontë's aim has been partly to show us the immeasurable gulf between his outward appearances (what I have called his 'masks') and the primitive world in which his lost soul strives to live. The 'brute' or 'fiend' whom we have come to detest is indeed scarcely human; on the one hand, a mechanical intelligence trying to carry out a purpose which grows less real the nearer it is to fulfilment; on the other, an animal inflicting torment on others in order to forget its own torment. His mind, he says, 'is so eternally secluded in itself' (XXXIII) and his heart is 'an earthly hell'.

[1] Cf. Catherine's remark to Nelly in X: 'I stand between him [Hindley] and bodily harm.'
[2] In soldering the window to prevent a further escape by Cathy, he need have no fear now of shutting Catherine out.

2. The Frost Set In (XXX-XXXI)

In these chapters the living are yoked with the dead, and the dominant images in Zillah's unfeeling narrative are those of coldness and death.[1] Human sympathy at the Heights reaches its lowest ebb. If Cathy does not care to look after Linton, let her 'lock him up and leave him', says Heathcliff. And she complains, 'You have left me so long, to struggle against death alone, that I feel and see only death! I feel like death!'

Since he saw Catherine's dead face, Heathcliff too can 'feel and see only death'. The only time he shows even slight interest in Cathy[2] is at the moment of Linton's death, since she has now lived with death herself and all feelings in her are 'benumbed'. He then orders Joseph to 'remove the body to his chamber', and for two weeks afterwards the whole household treats Cathy as if she too were dead—'nobody asked anything about her'. It is only the cold which forces her, against her will, to return to the human society of the warm sitting-room.

Lockwood's parting visit to the Heights (XXXI) leaves the action static and suspended—'Oh! I'm tired—I'm *stalled*, Hareton!' Lockwood's shallow romanticism and humour reduce the situation (though it is still unresolved) to the status of a familiar fact, no longer mysterious: 'Mr. Heathcliff, grim and saturnine, on the one hand, and Hareton, absolutely dumb, on the other.'

But there are two new elements here which help to prepare us for the sequel: the 'restless, anxious expression' in Heathcliff's countenance which Lockwood 'had never remarked before', and the bitter recriminations between Cathy and Hareton. The theme of Cathy's antipathy to Hareton (with hints of an attraction between them) has given us a counterpoint to the main narrative of her dealings with the Heights; and the figure of the 'brute' Hareton, fundamentally sensitive and good-natured, has constantly grown in stature. He represents the old Earnshaw stock and Joseph has always stood up for him. Now Cathy's educating him with 'tales and poetry' (particularly ballads—an excellent syllabus for a backward reader!) is placed in the foreground of the story. By this means, Cathy is restored to the world of the living and Hareton's 'uncultivated feelings' are refined. The Heights are gradually humanised.

[1] Cp. the air of the Heights at the end of III, 'cold as impalpable ice'.
[2] 'Now—Catherine,' he said, 'how do you feel?'

9. The Narrative Form, II

1. The Deepened Attraction

We were prepared for the transition from Nelly back to Lockwood in XXXI by the unwinding of the action and by the interposing between the two of Zillah (whom Lockwood met in II and whose narrative takes place six weeks before his first arrival). Zillah is useful not so much as a stop-gap, but because, like Lockwood, she is a comparative outsider to the Heights: through her, Nelly's story can become disengaged.

This may be the best point to consider Lockwood's function as a listener. Nelly's story is arranged in three sections: the first two 'sittings' are divided by the dialogue with Lockwood in VII, and the third (after the interlude at the beginning of X) is supposed to be transcribed by Lockwood from several sittings, as nearly as possible in Nelly's own words.

The dialogue in VII has a more important function than that of justifying Nelly's ability as a storyteller. It is necessary that Lockwood should have his say, and so speak for the reader too. His patronising tone, with its air of critical detachment, puts us at our ease, and enables him to explain the fascination her story has for him: '. . . the deepened attraction is not entirely owing to the situation of the looker-on. They *do* live more in earnest, more in themselves, and less in surface change, and frivolous external things. I could fancy a love for life here almost possible . . .', etc.

In thus acknowledging the spell he is under and modifying the superficial attitudes he had adopted at first, he helps us to 'suspend our disbelief' and makes it easier for us to give way, as he does, to Nelly's growing ascendancy. This dialogue, like that with the Wedding Guest in *The Ancient Mariner*, is an essential part of the convention which allows the 'inner' story of the past to come out of its frame and take command.

But Lockwood still has important functions to fulfil: so the remaining short breaks remind us that he is still there recovering from illness, and mark the passage of present time through the winter of 1801.

2. Time and the Law

The year 1801 is the story's *terminus a quo* and *terminus ad quem* up to this point, as is September 1802 of its sequel. To mark the passage of past time in relation to this date, Nelly's story has been studded with brief indications of the dating of events. In fact it is possible to work out from these indications the precise dates of all the main events, including the ages of the protagonists and, in some cases, the day of the week.[1]

A graph of the novel's time-structure (with the pages marked vertically, and the dates from 1771-1802 marked horizontally) is useful in showing the novel's structure—though it must be remembered that it does not show Brontë's perspective of different events, her arrangement of foreground and background and her shifts back and forth, over short periods of time.

However, it does reveal the following features clearly: The only sudden jumps from present to distant past are Catherine's diary (III), the beginning of Nelly's story (IV) and Heathcliff's second narrative (XXIX). Excluding the period before Mr. Earnshaw's death, the treatment of Catherine's history corresponds quite closely in general pattern to that of Cathy's—long, full accounts of particular days or weeks of intense activity, followed by sudden jumps forward. The long gap following Linton's removal to the Heights (XX) corresponds to that following Heathcliff's disappearance (IX), and the time-sequence leading to the climax of the Cathy/Linton relationship corresponds closely with that leading up to Catherine's death. But the graph of Cathy's history is 'shallower' than her mother's: it ranges over a much shorter period of time.

Besides this parallelism in the treatment of the two generations, Brontë's precise dating has another importance. In a story where so much takes place at close quarters in immense 'foreground' sequences of a few hours or days, and where there are gaps and time shifts, we might tend to ignore the minor incidents and connections. But this is a 'history' of two families, whose involved fate is working itself out over three generations. It must be made of resistant material: we must be made aware of the passage of years and of the complex 'plot' behind its drama. With these strong links Brontë is free to highlight the most critical events in the lives of Heathcliff and Catherine. By her precise plotting, she succeeds in making us feel the lapse of time without cluttering her story with dates, and holds an involved family history together[2] with-

---

[1] This has been done meticulously (but with a few errors) by C.P.S. in *The Structure of Wuthering Heights* (University Microfilms, Inc.).

[2] Cp., in this, George Eliot's *Felix Holt* or *Daniel Deronda*.

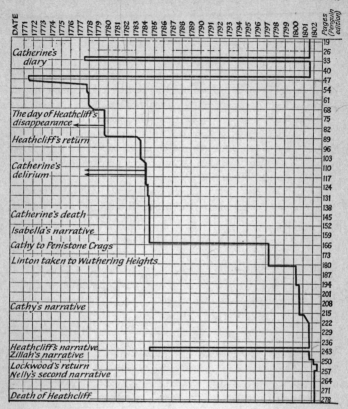

out losing the dramatic tension and excitement of an adventure story. For similar reasons, the topography and botany are precise and correct. The same applies to the legal background to Heathcliff's acquiring of both properties. It has been shown conclusively[1] that Brontë's knowledge of the law was at least equal to Jane Austen's, and that the working out of her plot depended on a full understanding of Inheritance Acts, Wills Acts, and the law of entails. Thus Brontë has ensured that the historical basis for her novel is accurate, though (unlike

[1] C.P.S., op. cit.

D

Felix Holt) it contains very few legal terms or explanations. We can ignore such details if we choose; if we care to look into them, we shall find them all consistent.[1]

3. *The Last Drop of Poison*

M. Héger, Brontë's Belgian teacher, praised her as much for her powers of logic as for her historical imagination. She should, he said, have been 'a great navigator, deducing new spheres from a knowledge of the old . . . or a great historian, using her strong imagination and sense of logic to present scenes and characters and opinions so powerfully as to convince her readers, whatever their previous judgements and cooler perceptions of the truth.'

Consider, for example, the remarkable symmetry in the family tree of the Lintons and Earnshaws, and the use Brontë makes of this in her plot:

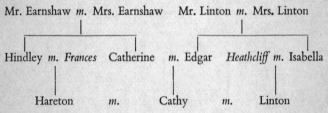

Mr. Earnshaw *m.* Mrs. Earnshaw   Mr. Linton *m.* Mrs. Linton

Hindley *m. Frances* Catherine *m.* Edgar   *Heathcliff m.* Isabella

Hareton   *m.*   Cathy   *m.*   Linton

Though the structure is symmetrical (with the two 'foreigners', Heathcliff and Frances, occupying similar positions on each side), the actual balance of strength is weighted on the side of the Earnshaws—the yeoman farmers being more fit to survive than the landed gentry. For Heathcliff, who is out of place in the pedigree of the Lintons, adds nothing to the strength of their stock, and the final issue leaves Hareton and Cathy heirs to both properties.

A similar inexorable but biassed logic is shown in Brontë's working out of the theme of retributive justice and expiation. In one of her essays written for M. Héger, she expressed her belief that before happiness could be attained, evil must exhaust itself through suffering in this world:

'God is the God of justice and mercy; then, assuredly, each pain that

[1] 'So far as I know', writes C.P.S., 'there is no other novel in the world which it is possible to subject to an analysis of the kind I have tried to make.'

he inflicts on his creatures, *be they human or animal, rational or irrational*, each suffering of our unhappy nature is only a seed for that divine harvest which will be gathered when *sin having spent its last drop of poison, death having thrown its last dart*, both will expire on the funeral pyre of a universe in flame, and will leave their former victims to an eternal realm of happiness and glory.'[1] (My italics.)

This passage suggests so many lines of interpretation for the novel, that it may be best here to leave every reader to make what use of it he can: to observe, for instance, how the biblical teaching 'Vengeance is mine, I will repay, saith the Lord' is repeatedly echoed; how each character undergoes a purgatory of isolation fitted to his or her own sins and the weaknesses of each family (this especially applying to those, like Hindley and Heathcliff, who take the divine prerogative into their own hands);[2] how the original sins of the parents leave a legacy of woe for their children, and through Catherine's pride, this burden is passed on to the third generation; and how close Cathy comes to committing the same sin of pride in her relationship with Hareton.

Mr. Colman Kavanagh has worked this theme out according to a Christian pattern of ideas in his essay on *The Symbolism of Wuthering Heights*; and Mr. J. Hillis Miller, in his book *The Disappearance of God*, has done it more convincingly, taking into account the Calvinistic doctrines with which Brontë was familiar. Such patterns of meaning are certainly present in the novel, but whichever line we choose to follow, there will always be other patterns cutting across it. For in spite of Brontë's strong 'sense of logic', the 'meaning' of *Wuthering Heights* cannot be pinned down to any one system of beliefs.

10. *A Heaven in Hell's Despair*

1. *Uprooting the Currant Bushes (XXXII-XXXIII)*

The date 1802 at the head of XXXII marks the beginning of a new narrative cycle, a brief sequel to the first, similar in structure but quite

[1] See Suggestions for Further Critical Study, p. 70.
[2] Cf. Nelly in VI: 'For shame, Heathcliff! It is for God to punish wicked people . . .', etc.

different in mood and direction. Again Lockwood comes to Gimmerton by chance, and the weather and landscape present an idyllic aspect which draws him to the Heights. But instead of a chained gate, he finds open doors and lattices; instead of gruff voices, the voices of lovers—Cathy's 'as sweet as a silver bell' answered by Hareton's 'deep but softened tones'. The effect on him of this changed atmosphere is something like that of Wordsworth's 'gentle shock of mild surprise'—carrying a hint of the full significance of his 'perfect misanthropist's heaven' in the landscape's luminous clarity, the fragrance of stocks and wallflowers, the red light from the fire and the overheard dialogue of the lovers. Then he hears the news of Heathcliff's death and we are plunged into the 'sequel of Mr. Heathcliff's history'.

Nelly begins with the love story. The almost praeternatural beauty of the landscape[1] as Lockwood climbs the 'stony by-road'—with its reminder of Nelly's ecstasy (XI) and her words about the 'shadowless hereafter' (XVI)—makes the reader receptive to subtle changes while at the same time leading him to expect a romantic conclusion. We are waiting for Heathcliff to be disposed of quickly, to make way for Cathy and Hareton, whose courtship is like a charming version of Beauty and the Beast. In defiance of Joseph, the Heights is now turned into a flowery home. Cathy and Hareton uproot Joseph's currant-bushes, the hardy perennials of the Heights, planting in their place flowers 'imported from the Grange'; and instead of reading 'T'Broad Road to Destruction', Cathy educates Hareton with her favourite poems. On Easter Monday, the day of their reconciliation, Joseph is forced to 'gie up his own hearthstun'.

But in the meantime, what of Heathcliff? How is his 'hell' to be assimilated into this fragile 'heaven'? The situation is rather as if he were being asked to sit and look on while Perdita made daisy-chains for Florizel, wishing to marry her 'gentler scion' to his 'wildest stock'. Can 'great creating Nature'—the half-cultivated nature of a Cathy or a Perdita—win over a Heathcliff? Brontë has set herself a difficult problem.

By a subtle shifting of tones, interweaving the story of Cathy and Hareton with the hollow sound of the approaching maelstrom, the romance is used to bring us back to Heathcliff. The lovers dare not laugh

---

[1] The combination of sinking sun and rising moon has an obvious 'symbolic' significance. The moon so illuminates the landscape that Lockwood 'could see every pebble on the path, and every blade of grass'.

at table even when Hareton puts primroses in Cathy's porridge, because they are hypnotised by Heathcliff's taut, oppressive silence. The atmosphere gradually becomes as tense and nervous as the dreary comedy of Vladimir and Estragon, all natural human reactions being inhibited. We know that he could at any time destroy their happiness at a single blow.

The shift of focus from Cathy and Hareton to Heathcliff is brought about through the expression of their eyes. At every moment, their eyes turn anxiously to him. One glance from his black eyes silences them. At the moment when he is about to strike Cathy, he suddenly looks into her eyes, pauses, and unaccountably releases her. When he unexpectedly returns to the house at dusk, Cathy and Hareton simultaneously raise their eyes to encounter his. Heathcliff seems disarmed—and at this point Nelly reminds us that their eyes are those of Catherine Earnshaw. This is enough. Heathcliff waves them away as if they did not exist. Before we know it, we are swept up again into Heathcliff's passion—'for what is not connected with her to me? and what does not recall her? I cannot look down to this floor but her features are shaped in the flags! In every cloud, in every tree—filling the air at night, and caught by glimpses in every object by day—I am surrounded with her image. . . . The entire world is a dreadful collection of memoranda that she did exist, and that I have lost her! Well, Hareton's aspect was the ghost of my immortal love; of my wild endeavours to hold my right; my degradation, my pride, my happiness, and my anguish.'

The bonds that have held our sympathy back and kept Heathcliff's mysterious passion so long in check are at last broken. Through the mounting eloquence of his dialogue with Nelly, his stature is raised to that of a tragic hero. The love of Cathy and Hareton was, after all, only a means of leading us to the moment of Heathcliff's self-discovery, the turning-point of great tragedy which makes us see a Macbeth or a Heathcliff, with all their brutality, as suffering human beings who can no longer control their fate. Like Macbeth, Heathcliff comes at last to see the futility of all his 'violent exertions'. But Heathcliff has not even the power to defy his fate: he 'can't take the trouble to raise a hand' against his enemies.

2. The Open Lattice (XXXIV)

In so far as Brontë's art is one of 'bringing the unreal world too strangely near',[1] this final chapter is her greatest achievement. No longer

[1] From the poem quoted as an epigraph on p. 65.

making use of long, rhetorical speeches, she presents the 'strange change' in Heathcliff entirely in dramatic form, through Nelly's precise observation of his expressions and movements. The style combines a concrete particularity equal to Defoe's with the subtle suggestiveness and effect of shock which Henry James uses in *The Turn of the Screw*. There is, therefore, nothing particularly 'spooky', no false inducement of mystery here or anywhere in the novel. Our attention is concentrated chiefly on physical symptoms—the unnatural smile and 'joyful glitter' in Heathcliff's eyes, his pallid face, the 'strong thrilling, rather than trembling' of his body, 'as a tight-stretched cord vibrates', his breathing as fast as a cat's, and his stealthy preoccupied comings and goings. So the impression of an immense spiritual change is conveyed in a few compressed pages. We are made to feel palpably the tension in him ('it is like bending back a stiff spring').

We are not told what he does when he leaves the house, or what happened that first night to 'alter the aspect of his whole face'. We only see the changes in him when he returns, and sense from his breathless answers that he is under some unbearable strain ('utterly too much for flesh and blood to bear'). His case is for the reader to diagnose. But Brontë, with her half-concealed sense of logic, has so planted the clues that we connect them with other facts contained in earlier 'recesses' of the novel; and these associations are so firmly established in our imagination that we are forced towards a predetermined conclusion.

It is especially important here, as in XV, to grasp precisely what happens. Heathcliff's strange 'disorder' and starvation (like Catherine's in XII) lasts for four days, each of which brings fresh developments. All this time, Nelly's excited curiosity increases, till on the third and fourth nights she is in a state of sleepless agitation and superstitious dread. The narrative in this case owes much of its intensity to Nelly's emotional involvement: her nightly fears bring back relevant memories of Heathcliff's past life, and the fascination he exercises over her causes her to note all the crucial objects (especially windows) that determine our response. We take a pleasure in spotting significances which she misses; and in thus prompting us to interpret events for ourselves, Brontë ensures that we grasp the meaning of those images which were formerly equivocal. So our picture of the novel's central themes and actions reaches finality.

We should notice particularly the play on the indoor and outdoor worlds, and the sequence of mornings, evenings and nights with their

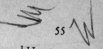

different effects of light and weather. We begin with Cathy and Hareton outdoors on a morning of 'spring fragrance', sweet and warm. Then Heathcliff returns from his night out of doors in strange excitement, and we move inside. He 'looks eagerly towards the window' and goes out again, leaving his meal untouched. In the afternoon, we find him leaning with his back to 'an open lattice' and glaring into the gloom of the parlour. At this point, the sound of Gimmerton beck is heard from a great distance with exaggerated clarity, and we are reminded of a similar allusion to it in XV, when Catherine sat in a trance just before Heathcliff burst in upon her. In this way the sense of her spirit's presence is first conveyed—the clarity of the beck hinting at her unclouded life, at one with nature, which Heathcliff will soon share.

Nelly then shuts the casements, but when she comes to the one where Heathcliff stands, she suddenly sees him as a goblin and runs away in a 'state of dread'. (The same thing happened when he appeared on the door-stones in XI—'I ran down the road . . . as scared as if I had raised a goblin.')

On this, the second night, Heathcliff retires, not to his usual room, but to that with the panelled bed which, we remember, he had long ago been 'beaten out of' by Catherine's spirit. Prompted partly by Lockwood's 'nightmare', he appears to have returned to the state of mind he was in on the night of Catherine's burial, when he expected to see her in that room. Nelly's 'tracking his existence over again' during the same night now recalls to us the course of his whole life, from the moment when he first came to the Heights, 'a dark little thing, harboured by a good man to his bane'. So the mystery of his origin ('a gift of God . . .', etc.) is linked with that of his final destiny.

The second day gives us the extraordinary scene of his 'gazing at something within two yards' distance'. His experience is one of both bliss and agony: there is no half-way between his hell and his heaven— 'Last night I was on the threshold of hell. Today, I am within sight of my heaven. I have my eyes on it: hardly three feet separate me!'[1]

On the third night he appears to be pleading desperately with Cather-ine. But he still clings to life: he asks Nelly to light him a fire, and protests to her: 'It is not my fault that I cannot eat or rest.' He is certainly *not* starving himself or acting 'through settled designs': he is being *acted upon*. In fact he still hopes to reach his goal in this life—'I must reach it

---

[1] Mr. Derek Stanford possibly said more than he meant when he re-marked of Heathcliff: 'The broad middle register of the human, he misses.'

first, and then I'll rest.' But his concern about his will and burial shows that he now suspects he may soon have to die to attain '*his* heaven'—one to which Nelly's Christian notions of sin and repentance have no relevance.

On the third day he shows the fear and loneliness of his ordeal: 'he wanted somebody with him'. From his last words ('By God! she's relentless . . .', etc.) we know that he believes Catherine is *driving* him, through starvation and sleeplessness, to the death which is the condition of his reaching her. The will to live (his strongest instinct from the beginning), which is connected (XXXIII) with his immensely strong physical constitution, is being destroyed with his body.

On the fourth night he is resigned to death at last. So he cuts himself off from all 'society' for good by locking himself in the room with the panelled bed, and opens the lattice. (Catherine also locked herself in to starve herself, begging Nelly to open the casement to give her 'a chance of life'.) Whenever Catherine's spirit has become palpable, there has been a storm of rain or snow. So when Nelly finds Heathcliff dead 'his face and throat were washed with rain' and 'the bedclothes dripped'. Here again is the image of the open lattice, now 'flapping to and fro', since whether it is closed or open no longer matters. As it swings, it grazes his skin—but there is no more drawing of blood at the pane, for Heathcliff has gone beyond the world of enchantment and superstition. He is in Catherine's 'glorious world' where 'life is boundless in its duration, and love in its sympathy, and joy in its fullness' (XVI).

Nelly's account of her finding Heathcliff dead—concise, visual, rhythmically taut—completes our varied impressions of him: the 'stratified layers' of his history are seen now as a single escarpment. The words 'His eyes met mine so keen and fierce' are the counterpart to the withdrawn black eyes of the novel's opening, and to Nelly's 'couple of black fiends, so deeply buried, who never open their windows boldly, but lurk glinting under them, like devils' spies' (VII). But now he is dead, his eyes look out with a 'life-like gaze of exultation' and 'will not shut'.[1] In death he is still demonic, as he seemed to Isabella. The 'sharp

---

[1] Cp., too, Isabella's description of him (XVII): 'basilisk eyes . . . nearly quenched by sleeplessness . . . lips . . . devoid of their ferocious sneer . . . his eyes rained down tears among the ashes . . . I stared full at him. . . . The clouded windows of hell flashed a moment towards me; the fiend which usually looked out, however, was . . . dimmed and drowned . . .', etc.

white teeth' still sneering remind us of the 'sharp cannibal teeth' of XVII, when his 'black countenance looked blightingly through' the window he had smashed, and 'his hair and clothes were whitened with snow'.

D. H. Lawrence saw in the cruelty of the Mexican Indians a genuine religious impulse, in tune with their savage landscape—an impulse for union with the whole of creation. So Brontë has succeeded in making us feel that Heathcliff's rapacity is part of a real yearning for an eternity of life, which in the end is fulfilled.

Heathcliff's triumph of single-mindedness[1] has made possible the earthly happiness of Cathy and Hareton, the reconciliation of the two houses and the restoration to its rights of the 'ancient Earnshaw stock'. (Hareton's 'streaming face' as he covers Heathcliff's grave is an unconscious tribute to his master's strength, and a recognition of his humanity—for Heathcliff had a genuine feeling for Hareton.) But the restoration of the old order is far from complete. The flowers from the Grange will not permanently replace Joseph's currants. The ghosts of Catherine and Heathcliff inherit the Heights, and (here is Brontë's ironic *coup de grâce* to those who look for a romantic resolution) Joseph is to live on there, in the lair of his kitchen, while the rest of the house is to be shut up.

So the human figures are finally withdrawn, each assimilated into its natural background. Even the stranger Lockwood is absorbed in the life of nature, for it is he who now draws us away from the 'grim house' into the harmony of the landscape, whose storms have ravaged the kirk, and which even now is instinct with life. In the last sentence, the souls of the dead seem still to be present in the fluttering moths and the soft wind. 'Heath' and 'harebells' echo the names 'Heathcliff' and 'Hareton', and the rhythm is so delicately and ambiguously poised as to express a strange unquiet amid the stillness.

[1] 'I have a single wish, and my whole being and faculties are yearning to attain it. They have yearned towards it so long, and so unwaveringly, that I'm convinced it *will* be reached—and soon—because it has devoured my existence. . . .' (XXXIII)

11. *The Circumambient Universe*

Wuthering Heights is profoundly informed with the attitudes of
'animism', by which the natural world . . . appears to act with an
energy similar to the energies of the soul.
      Dorothy Van Ghent, *The English Novel, Form and Function*

1. *Egdon Heath and the Blackhorse Marsh*

In considering the question of the 'otherness' of the world of nature to
human life, it is useful to read Hardy's *The Return of the Native* with
Wuthering Heights. The two books are alike in having an extremely
localised setting—remote houses squatting in the great spaces of a wild
heathland country—but very different in the use they make of it. By
comparing them we may gain a clearer understanding of the differences
between Brontë's vision of the world and that of other nineteenth-
century novelists of rural or provincial life.[1]

There could scarcely be a greater contrast than that between Brontë's
opening chapters and Hardy's. Hardy leads us slowly, meditatively,
through brooding description and the building up of 'atmosphere' into
the scene of his story. Having first established the dark, primeval quality
of the heath, he places his human figures, one by one, in the landscape.
Its vastness is not merely one of extent: the ancient earthwork of
Rainbarrow takes on a significance comparable to that of the house on
Brontë's Heights, and the nature of Egdon Heath is unfolded in an
enormous perspective of time—history and pre-history—as well as
space. Throughout Hardy's story, the human figures are dwarfed by this
landscape. They are frequently seen at a distance crawling across the
heath like insects. They walk slowly to their lonely meeting-places, their
festivities or their deaths, surrounded by the workings of a nature that
is quite inhuman.

In *Wuthering Heights* people seldom approach slowly, from a distance:
they are upon us at once, starting up from the landscape, larger than life.
In Brontë, as in Wordsworth, nature plays a part in deciding human
destinies, but it never reduces human affairs to insignificance. The loves

[1] For an interesting comparison between Brontë and George Eliot, see
Dorothy Van Ghent, op. cit., the chapter on *Adam Bede*.

and sorrows of Clym, Eustacia, Wildeve and Thomasin are puny in comparison with those of Heathcliff and Catherine. Even Isabella experiences a hatred and fear so powerful that, when she flees from the Heights in her thin dress she does not notice the sleet, but leaps and bounds for five miles with an energy that seems superhuman.[1]

Since Hardy's heath stands above and beyond human life, he frequently focusses our attention on it by set descriptions of its plant and animal life,[2] showing its ecology, its stealthy seasonal changes and the struggle of the heathmen to wrest from it a bare livelihood. In contrast to Brontë's vigorous action, the life Hardy depicts is laborious and slow-moving. The heath will not tolerate unregulated passion or romantic aspiration, and it therefore destroys Eustacia, the goddess of poetry with her 'godlike conceit'. 'To dwell on a heath without studying its meanings was like wedding a foreigner without learning his Language.'[3] Hardy's novel is a study of the heath's meanings as they affect the human community.

Hardy is always present as commentator within his novel, and he invests every natural image with symbolic meaning. In *Wuthering Heights*, places and people *are* what they symbolise; their meanings are inherent in the action and do not need to be drawn out. Every effect of natural phenomena—cold, heat, storm, sunshine—is felt both as a physical sensation and as a spiritual force belonging to the human drama.

Whereas the characters in *Wuthering Heights* speak with a direct attacking vehemence, the speech of the natives of Egdon is often indirect, and always grave and deliberate. Their tone is one of resignation: even Eustacia knows that the ways of the heath are stronger than her desires.

Hardy is also concerned with the relationship of individuals to the local community and to the whole 'commonwealth' of mankind and living things. He reveals this in the special value he gives to rustic speech and customs—the surviving pagan rituals of bonfires, mummers' plays and maypoles. *Wuthering Heights* has no such communal 'chorus' other

[1] Interesting comparisons can be drawn between this scene of Isabella's flight, Catherine's exposure to the thunderstorm (IX), and Eustacia's attempted flight on the 'Night of the Sixth of November', the climax to Hardy's tragedy, where Nature blots out human passion.

[2] Cp. the *dramatic* use made in *Wuthering Heights* of lapwings, moor game, plant and animal life.

[3] Heathcliff, too, was not originally a native of the Heights. How well, and to what purpose, has he studied its 'meanings'?

than Joseph (for whom a neighbour is another soul destined for perdition) and Zillah (the sole representative of Gimmerton, who is indifferent to the inmates of the two houses). And Nelly is seen as one of
the household, not as a villager.

The village of Gimmerton barely exists in Brontë's novel; and when
Hindley, Heathcliff, Isabella or Lockwood go beyond it, they disappear
into an 'outer darkness'. We do not find in Brontë the same interest in
social changes, or the life and work of rural England, as we find in Hardy.
The Heights is seldom thought of as a farm; neither the topography of
the Dales, nor their way of life, have the same *kind* of relevance to
Wuthering Heights as the West Country has to Hardy's novels, or the
Potteries to those of Arnold Bennett.

In *The Return of the Native*, the heath unites more than divides human
beings, creating a community out of scattered hamlets. The network of
paths which links these hamlets represents their communal tradition,
and this alone survives personal tragedies. But in *Wuthering Heights* the
moors isolate and divide, and only the strong, passionate individual
survives. When Heathcliff disappears, Joseph can say gloatingly, 'I's
niver wonder but he's at t'bothom of a bog-hoile' (IX). And when Nelly
is kidnapped for five nights, Zillah and her gossips in Gimmerton
complacently accept the story that she is 'sunk in the Blackhorse marsh'.
'You must have got on an island? And how long were you in the hole?'
(XXVIII); Nelly does not seem taken aback by Zillah's indifference.

2. The Two Houses

Wuthering Heights gains universality by the special values it gives to
every feature in a remote, provincial setting; and its chief features are the
two rival houses which are always in the foreground. In other novels
whose titles are the names of houses (*Mansfield Park*, *Bleak House*,
Howards End) those houses represent certain traditional values to which
all their events are to be in some way referred. Though the Heights,
considered as the family home of the Earnshaws, has something of this
symbolic function, under Heathcliff's domination it becomes much
more. It seems to be the home of all those natural forces, death-dealing or
life-giving, which it is built to withstand; the fate of the Lintons, as well
as the Earnshaws, depends on their relationship to it.

Lockwood explains the meaning of its name: 'a significant provincial
adjective, descriptive of *the atmospheric tumult to which its station is exposed*

in stormy weather'.[1] It is clearly no Castle of Otranto. Brontë takes pains to stress its ordinariness, its rude, provincial homeliness. But its chief characteristics are exposure to the power of the wind, and fortress-like strength.

Much is made in *Wuthering Heights* of this contrast between exposure and enclosure, the world within and the world outside, suggested by Lockwood's opening description. A great deal of the action has to do with doors and windows (whether open or closed) and the crossing of thresholds (going out or coming in). The Heights seems to depend for its survival on its isolation from the world beyond the moor: and all the main sources of conflict (Heathcliff, Frances, and the foreign luxuries of the Grange) originate from outside.

As the protagonists are repeatedly subjected to rain, wind and sun, the theme of exposure to the elements gains in depth and complexity throughout the novel. The tumult of the elements is associated with the tumult of supernatural forces which Heathcliff and Catherine are not afraid of. 'These spiritual powers', writes Mr. J. Hillis Miller, 'are immanent in nature, and identified with its secret life. The expression of this double life in *Wuthering Heights*, as in Emily Brontë's poems, is an ancient and primitive symbol: the wind.'[2] We should consider, too, how throughout the novel human beings are described, especially by Catherine and Heathcliff, in animal images, which Brontë uses as emblems of the breaking down of barriers between the animal and the human.

On the Heights, the effects of weather are unsoftened. At Thrushcross Grange they are always gentler, filtered and diluted. Heathcliff and Catherine, brought up in the wild exposure of the Heights, are deprived of all civilised comforts. But the Grange is a house of soft, clinging luxury whose inmates are guarded by servants and bulldogs. For Cathy it is a walled Eden, with Heathcliff a Satan tempting her from without. The typical view from the Grange is through an open, first-floor lattice,

---

[1] Wuther or Whither (O.N.), *dial.*, to move swiftly with force; to make a sullen roaring, as the wind; to throw or beat violently (*Chambers Twentieth Century Dictionary*). It is natural to associate this with the English verbs 'weather' and 'wither', which suggest both the destructive and the restorative effects of wind and sunshine.

[2] Op. cit. An examination of the use Brontë makes of images of light and darkness (especially the association of dusk with the supernatural, and the contrast between natural and artificial light—the candles of the Heights and glimmering tapers of the Grange) is equally suggestive.

from which Catherine looks beyond the walled gardens and courts into the idyllic glen with its murmuring beck, and on to the kirk and moor beyond, which hides 'Wuthering Heights' from sight. Thus the world outside is framed like a picture, and it is only when the story is set at the Grange that we are conscious of nature as a background, at one remove from human lives.

In Jane Austen's *Sense and Responsibility*, Marianne Dashwood's habit of taking solitary walks round the grounds of Cleveland is satirised as a self-conscious affectation, and her imprudence in getting her feet wet is punished by a serious illness. When Catherine exposes herself to the thunderstorm and sits all night on the settle in her wet clothes, she too is reproved by Nelly for her folly. But Nelly's common sense is often shown to be inadequate: it does not stand, like Jane Austen's, between actions and our judgement of them (notice in this case Catherine's answers to Hindley's questions). Jane Austen was concerned to uphold the fabric of civilised society, while Brontë simply shows us what life is like both with, and without, civilised refinements—close to nature, or cut off from it.

Given the conditions, we are convinced of the truth of Catherine's passion: her despair over the loss of Heathcliff weighs more heavily on her than her drenched garments. As often in *Wuthering Heights*, there is here a genuine interaction between human passion and natural phenomena. An uncontrollable passion draws her out of the defences of the house into the storm; the storm in turn drenches her to the skin and she brings its effects back into the house.

The elements of nature in *Wuthering Heights* are not merely symbols. The rain is the rain, and the sun the sun. The moor which is Catherine's heaven is not the symbol of her love for Heathcliff. Her love is the bedrock of her life, because with him she had experienced the wild, free life of the moor, and he shared its character: 'An unreclaimed creature, without refinement, without cultivation: an arid wilderness of furze and whinstone.'

The exposed wilderness of unreclaimed nature is, for Brontë, the rock beneath the cultivated soil of human life, from which all our passions are ultimately derived. The two houses show us two possible ways of living: the one rock-like, built on the Heights, a bastion against the weather yet perilously close to the wild elements; the other crouched in the cultivated valley and standing in a sheltered park.

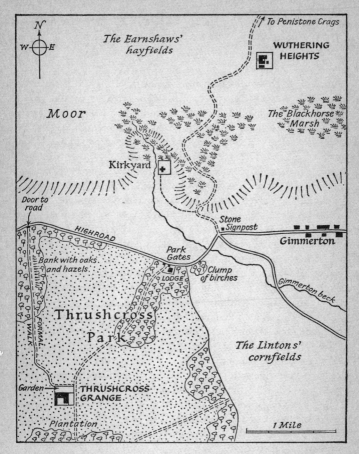

The Heights is a functional house: we are made aware of its architectural structure, within and without. Its roof 'had never been underdrawn: its entire anatomy lay bare to an enquiring eye' (I). But at no point are we given an architectural impression of the Grange. Instead, we look into its interior with Heathcliff and Catherine, and see it as 'a splendid place', rich, carpeted and cushioned with crimson. Decorated with delicate ornamentation in gold and silver and lit with soft, artificial light, it belongs to a 'civilisation' which values comfort more than life itself. Its children are spoiled and pampered so much that they are robbed of all connection with the sources of natural feeling.[1]

3. The Kirk

Apart from the two houses, there is one other important feature in Brontë's landscape—the kirk, sometimes referred to as Gimmerton 'chapel'. It stands about half-way between the two houses, on the edge of the moor. When Lockwood first introduces it to us in III, he describes its situation, close to a swamp which embalms the corpses in the church-yard, and tells us why, in 1801, it had no pastor.

Before the death of Frances, the Earnshaws had been regular church-goers and the curate, Shielders, had educated their children. Soon after her death, the curate stopped calling, and in XI the child Hareton tells Nelly: 'I was told the curate should have his —— teeth dashed down his —— throat, if he stepped over the threshold. . . .' The Lintons also had attended church; but after Catherine's death, though Cathy went to the 'chapel' occasionally, Edgar ceased to attend, for his grief trans-formed him 'into a complete hermit' (XVII). He only visited the churchyard in order to lie on the green mound of Catherine's grave, on every anniversary of her death.

Thus the church itself diminishes in importance until, on his last visit, Lockwood finds it falling into decay. For Catherine, to the surprise of the villagers, had chosen to be buried, not in the chapel, under the carved monuments of the Lintons, but 'on a green slope in the corner of the kirkyard, where the wall is so low that heath and bilberry plants have climbed over it from the moor; and the peat-mould almost buries it' (XVI). So for Edgar and Heathcliff, the masters of the two houses, this grave takes the place of the kirk as a centre of devotion, and the tradi-tional Christianity of the parish, once common to the Lintons and the Earnshaws, is superseded.

[1] Notice, in this connection, the important references to books and reading throughout the novel. For the children of the Heights, books provide an essential means of cultivation—Heathcliff's deterioration is largely due to his failure to 'keep up an equality with Catherine in her studies . . . he yielded with poignant though silent regret . . .', etc. But to those at the Grange, books only provide a means of escape: we associate them with heartlessness and lack of spirit (XII and elsewhere).

4. Worlds of Heaven and Hell

> What have those lonely mountains worth revealing?
> More glory and more grief than I can tell:
> The earth that wakes *one* human heart to feeling
> Can centre both the worlds of Heaven and Hell.
>   Attributed to Emily Brontë[1]

It is useful in interpreting *Wuthering Heights* to consider the frequent use in it of the words 'heaven' and 'hell' and other terms of salvation and damnation. The ready-to-hand hyperbole of heaven and hell had been overworked, especially in love-poetry, before Brontë's time,[2] and only a handful of English poets and dramatists (Marlowe, Shakespeare, Milton and Blake among them) had ever added much to the imaginative impact of these words. But in *Dr. Faustus*[3] and *Paradise Lost*, for example, the words derive their force largely from the assumption that heaven and hell exist, as objective, theological facts. In Brontë, the theological facts appear to exist only as shadows of Victorian hypocrisy; the reality to which they refer varies from person to person. The novel's whole pattern is designed to convince us that Heathcliff is *not* talking nonsense when he says, speaking of his own burial: 'No minister need come; nor need anything be said over me—I tell you I have nearly attained *my* heaven; and that of others is altogether unvalued and uncoveted by me.'

Throughout the novel's intricate pattern, a number of private heavens and hells are contrasted, each throwing the others into sharper relief. They intersect one another at many points—the distorted 'circles' of an Inferno-cum-Paradiso centred on Heathcliff and Catherine.

There is, first, Lockwood's 'perfect misanthropist's heaven'. On his final visit to the Heights, this landscape (which he has not seen before in summer) does indeed appear, as he puts it, 'divine'. It is transfigured by the love of Cathy and Hareton, and he now looks upon their romance

---

[1] Hadfield (*Collected Poems of Emily Brontë*) thinks that this poem, 'Often rebuked, yet always back returning', was written by Charlotte to express her thoughts about her sister.

[2] Cf. Scott's 'Love is heaven, and heaven is love' in *The Lay of the Last Minstrel*.

[3] Cf. 'Hell hath no limits, nor is circumscribed . . .', etc. (*Dr. Faustus*, 560).

with a pang of envy. Since he has not himself experienced the 'purgatory' of the Heights at first hand, as Cathy has, it is a 'heaven' in which he can have no permanent place.

Brontë uses the Latinate 'paradise', 'elysium', etc., only for the comparatively trivial or selfish contentments of those who are incapable of a greater happiness. So, for example, Hindley sits with Frances in his 'paradise' by the hearth, while Heathcliff and Catherine create their own 'heaven' together. We have noticed, too, that behind Nelly's religiosity there lies a fairy land of childhood which she passes on to Cathy through her 'nursery lore'; and that from this Cathy creates the Wordsworthian 'heaven' of her childhood. This is directly contrasted with Linton's drowsy heaven, which is really 'infantile' in the modern sense. Thus Cathy: ' "This is something like your paradise," said she, making an effort at cheerfulness',—and a few minutes later, 'I can't tell why we should stay. He's asleep. . . .' (XXVI)

Joseph's private heaven in the kitchen, far more solid and indestructible, is described in this way: 'Joseph seemed sitting in a sort of elysium alone, beside a roaring fire; a quart of ale on the table near him, bristling with large pieces of toasted oat-cake; and his black, short pipe in his mouth.' Since first exiled from the family sitting-room after Mr. Earnshaw's death, he has refused to admit that the Heights affords any civilised comforts other than the kitchen with its porridge, and the garrets with their sacks of malt and grain—the coarse essentials of life which he shares with Hareton: ' "*Parlour!*" he echoed sneeringly, "*parlour*! Nay, we've noa *parlours*. . . ." ' (XIII—Isabella's letter provides the best material for the study of Joseph.)

Though originally a usurper, Joseph grows in stature, becoming the upholder of the old Earnshaw tradition—his rough oatmeal-hospitality opposed to all refinements. He instils into Hareton a pride of name and lineage (XVII), and though driven in the end from his own 'hearthstun', he is reinstated at last as Hareton's tenant, as if in recognition of his strength and persistence. We see his tenacity most clearly in Isabella's narrative (XVII). Heathcliff pushes him on to his knees to mop up Hindley's blood, he joins his hands, begins to pray and then rises, vowing he will go to the Grange at once to fetch Mr. Linton, the magistrate. So obstinate is his defiance of Heathcliff, that his master is forced on to the defensive. Thus his 'elysium', though selfish, is not represented to us as wholly unscrupulous. It is a way of life fit to survive (Joseph keeps the farm-work going); and the Heights without Joseph would scarcely live in our imagination as a real household.

For Isabella, on the other hand, the Heights proves a sterile 'purgatory' inciting her only to hatred. But to Cathy it is a fruitful one, making possible her love for Hareton. For Hindley, too, the Heights becomes a real hell. Deprived of Frances, and having no better religion than Joseph's to support him, he falls into frenzied despair: 'He neither wept nor prayed; he cursed and defied: execrated God and man, and gave himself up to reckless dissipation' (VIII). His speeches are filled with the language of perdition.

Hindley's conventional form of despair is deliberately set against Edgar's equally conventional expressions of hope and trust in God's providence. Nelly, who speaks for Edgar in matters of religious sentiment, makes this contrast explicit: 'I used to draw a comparison between him and Hindley. . . . One hoped, and the other despaired: they chose their lots, and were righteously doomed to endure them. . . .' This complacently homiletic language suits them both; for Hindley's curses only reveal his helplessness, while Edgar's sanctity (he dies blissfully, like a saint) is as ineffectual as Hindley's blasphemy. Both lose all they possess to the wiles of Heathcliff.

5. The Peat-mould

No more need be said here of the heavens and hells of Catherine and Heathcliff, since this commentary has been largely concerned with them. Lying in the peat-mould after her death, Catherine exercises a greater power than she did in life. As the story progresses, Edgar's thoughts, no less than Heathcliff's, become centred on the kirkyard. His longing to share her death (in a sense, he is ahead of Heathcliff in this) easily takes away the importance for him of his social functions as a landed gentleman, a magistrate and a parishioner of Gimmerton. Catherine's spirit, still alive in the earth and on the Heights, draws first Edgar, then Heathcliff, into its own 'heaven', which belongs to the world of nature, above and beyond the kirk: 'It's a rough journey, and a sad heart to travel it; and we must pass by Gimmerton Kirk, to go that journey! We've braved its ghosts often together, and dared each other to stand among the graves and ask them to come. But, Heathcliff, if I dare you now, will you venture? If you do, I'll keep you. I'll not lie there by myself: they may bury me twelve feet deep, and throw the church down over me, but I won't rest till you are with me. I never will!'

So Catherine's 'green slope', where Lockwood stands at the end of the novel, is a symbol of the final harmony which Nature's economy has woven out of the conflicting heavens and hells. In the decay of the kirk itself, we see the decay of Victorian Christianity. And the grave 'half buried beneath the heath', where Catherine lies at peace between Edgar and Heathcliff, is the sign that her rebellion against God's providence has triumphed at last: she has passed by Gimmerton Kirk, and found again, with Heathcliff, her 'heaven' in the middle of the moor.

6. An Absolute Hierarchy

Nature is thus seen in the novel as a complex of spiritual forces, embodying all that can be apprehended of fate and the supernatural. Its workings are beyond good and evil in the social and moral sense. Only that which is strong and instinct with passionate feeling survives: Brontë's nature has no place for cold-hearted sentiment, softness, kindly religiosity or conventional moralism.

The setting of the novel is such that lawlessness and superstition lie close to the edge of an imperilled civilisation, where two decaying religious traditions, one sentimentally pietistic, the other crudely Calvinistic, give rise to the dominant images of Heaven and Hell. The traditional, biblical language is caught up in a drama of violent passion and pre-Christian belief, which carries it very far from its original moorings. In place of a traditional Christianity and its social values, different forms of animism—savagely heathen or limpidly Wordsworthian—spring to life, passions of love and vengeance being expressed in a language that is partly a revivification of the old religious jargons, and partly that of a newly-animated nature-worship.

Yet in *Wuthering Heights*, human passions are always seen as coexisting with their opposites: the dictates of a homely common sense surround every outburst of feeling; and love, which gives rise to hatred and cruelty, triumphs in a story which lacks the element of Rousseau-like sentiment, and whose circumstances preclude affectation.

Brontë may lead us to question whether there is any one natural and social order, the same for all men and women. The conflicting individual heavens and hells confront one another at every turn: incompatible ways of life, coupled in grotesque ways which sometimes lead to violence and hysteria, sometimes to lifeless neutrality and sometimes to new and fuller forms of life. Yet the novel is instinct with a sense of life's intensity and resilience, even defiance, in the face of misery and death. It makes no exclusive moral judgements, except, perhaps, one of hostility towards all complacent assumptions and artificial schemes of salvation. It leaves us with a host of unanswered questions and embodies no consistent philosophy of life. But its perfection of form is such that every event seems inevitable, and its subjective heavens and hells are raised to a level of universality.

The quality in Brontë which we have been trying to define has perhaps been summed up best by Mr. G. D. Klingopoulos, who had this to say of *Wuthering Heights*:

'It has anonymity. It is not complete. Perhaps some ballads represent it in English, but it seldom appears in the main stream, and few writers are in touch with it. It is a quality of experience the expression of which is at once an act of despair and an act of recognition or of worship. It is the recognition of an absolute hierarchy. This is also the feeling in Aeschylus. It is found amongst genuine peasants and is a great strength. Developing in places which yield only the permanent essentials of experience, it is undistracted and universal.'[1]

[1] *The Novel as Dramatic Poem*: 'Wuthering Heights', *Scrutiny*, xiv, 4 (1946-7).

Suggestions for Further Critical Study

1. Comparison

Jane Austen, *Sense and Sensibility*

Walter Scott, *Guy Mannering; The Black Dwarf*

Charlotte Brontë, *Jane Eyre*

V. H. Collins (editor), *Ghosts and Marvels* (The World's Classics)

Thomas Hardy, *The Return of the Native*

Henry James, *The Turn of the Screw*

George Douglas Brown, *The House with the Green Shutters*

2. Background

Mario Praz, *The Romantic Agony*, esp. II ('The Metamorphoses of Satan')

Denis de Rougemont, *Passion and Society*

Philip Henderson (editor), *Selected Poems of Emily Brontë*

Emily Brontë, *Five Essays Written in French*, translated Lorine White Nigel (Texas University Press)

Fannie E. Ratchford, *The Brontë's Web of Childhood* (Columbia University Press)

—— *Gondal's Queen: A Novel in Verse by Emily Jane Brontë* (University of Texas Press)

Mrs. Gaskell, *The Life of Charlotte Brontë*, esp. Introduction and Chapters I and II

Charlotte Brontë, Preface to *Wuthering Heights* (Penguin Edition)

F. J. Child, *The English and Scottish Popular Ballads*

M. J. C. Hodgart, *The Ballads*

3. Criticism and Interpretation

E. M. Forster, *Aspects of the Novel*

Eric Auerbach, *Mimesis*, esp. Chapters I, II and XIII

Dorothy Van Ghent, *The English Novel, Form and Function*

J. Hillis Miller, *The Disappearance of God*

C.P.S., *The Structure of Wuthering Heights* (University Microfilms, Inc., Anne Arbor; London)

Colman Kavanagh, *The Symbolism of Wuthering Heights* (John Long, Ltd.)

Richard Chase, 'The Brontës, or Myth Domesticated' (*Forms in Modern Fiction*, edited Van O'Connor, University of Minnesota Press)

F. R. and Q. D. Leavis, *Lectures in America* (Chatto and Windus), contains an important essay on *Wuthering Heights* by Q. D. Leavis.

Index